MAGAZINE

delicious.

ONE-POT DISHES

HarperCollins*Publishers*
77–85 Fulham Palace Road,
Hammersmith, London W6 8JB
www.harpercollins.co.uk

First published by HarperCollins*Publishers* 2009

10 9 8 7 6 5 4 3

A catalogue record of this book is available from the British Library

ISBN-13 978-0-00-732836-9

Printed and bound in China by South China Printing Co. Ltd

contents

introduction

My favourite dishes are often those spooned from one steaming pan or pot that are a complete meal in themselves – or at least served with little more than a side dish of simply cooked potatoes, rice or seasonal vegetables. Think slow-cooked stews and casseroles, hearty soups or oven bakes and roasts, and you'll get the picture.

'One-pot' recipes are essentially cooked in and served from one pot or dish. For such recipes a large flameproof casserole is well worth investing in, as it makes the jump from hob to oven effortless. In many cases it also means that just one pot or pan is employed from start to finish, but in some recipes a bowl or another pan may come to the rescue to complete the dish. Whatever, you can be sure that the minimum amount of hassle and washing up awaits you in this collection of recipes.

Soups may seem obvious choices here, although the recipes are anything but; with gems like Moroccan spiced soup with jewelled couscous, prawn and Parmesan risotto soup and pasta and chickpea soup. Classic main courses like Lancashire hotpot, lamb Biryani and pork and pepper goulash are backed up by new takes on old favourites such as Mexican minced beef and spicy polenta cobbler, lemon roast chicken with peppers, and spicy meatball curry. You'll also find many of the dishes in this book are suitable for freezing, which is always welcome amongst busy households.

At delicious. magazine all the recipes are tested in our kitchen and we are satisfied that they will read, cook and taste to the highest standards, every time.

Matthew Drennan
delicious. Magazine Editor

Conversion tables

All the recipes in this book list only metric measurements (also used by Australian cooks). The conversions listed here are approximate for imperial measurements (also used by American cooks).

Oven temperatures

°C	Fan°C	°F	Gas	Description
110	90	225	¼	Very cool
120	100	250	½	Very cool
140	120	275	1	Cool
150	130	300	2	Cool
160	140	325	3	Warm
180	160	350	4	Moderate
190	170	375	5	Moderately hot
200	180	400	6	Fairly hot
220	200	425	7	Hot
230	210	450	8	Very hot
240	220	475	9	Very hot

Weights for dry ingredients

Metric	Imperial	Metric	Imperial
7g	¼oz	425g	15oz
15g	½oz	450g	1lb
20g	¾oz	500g	1lb 2oz
25g	1oz	550g	1¼lb
40g	1½oz	600g	1lb 5oz
50g	2oz	650g	1lb 7oz
60g	2½oz	675g	1½lb
75g	3oz	700g	1lb 9oz
100g	3½oz	750g	1lb 11oz
125g	4oz	800g	1¾lb
140g	4½oz	900g	2lb
150g	5oz	1kg	2¼lb
165g	5½oz	1.1kg	2½lb
175g	6oz	1.25kg	2¾lb
200g	7oz	1.35kg	3lb
225g	8oz	1.5kg	3lb 6oz
250g	9oz	1.8kg	4lb
275g	10oz	2kg	4½lb
300g	11oz	2.25kg	5lb
350g	12oz	2.5kg	5½lb
375g	13oz	2.75kg	6lb
400g	14oz	3kg	6¾lb

Liquid measures

Metric	Imperial	Aus	US
25ml	1fl oz		
50ml	2fl oz	¼ cup	¼ cup
75ml	3fl oz		
100ml	3½fl oz		
120ml	4fl oz	½ cup	½ cup
150ml	5fl oz		
175ml	6 fl oz	¾ cup	¾ cup
200ml	7fl oz		
250ml	8fl oz	1 cup	1 cup
300ml	10fl oz/½ pint	½ pint	1¼ cups
350ml	12fl oz		
400ml	14fl oz		
450ml	15fl oz	2 cups	2 cups/1 pint
600ml	1 pint	1 pint	2½ cups
750ml	1¼ pints		
900ml	1½ pints		
1 litre	1¾ pints	1¾ pints	1 quart
1.2 litres	2 pints		
1.4 litres	2½ pints		
1.5 litres	2¾ pints		
1.7 litres	3 pints		
2 litres	3½ pints		
3 litres	5¼ pints		

UK–Australian tablespoon conversions

1 x UK or Australian teaspoon is 5ml

1 x UK tablespoon is 3 teaspoons/15ml

1 Australian tablespoon is 4 teaspoons/20ml

soups

Fennel soup with winter greens and bacon

This warming soup is crammed with winter goodness and has a rich, satisfying flavour.

SERVES 4
READY IN ABOUT 1¼ HOURS

100g butter
2 large leeks, sliced and washed thoroughly
1 tsp fennel seeds, crushed
3 fennel bulbs, coarsely chopped
900g potatoes, roughly chopped
1.2 litres chicken stock, hot
150ml whipping cream

For the winter greens and bacon

1 small or ½ large Savoy cabbage or other winter greens
50g butter
175g pancetta or smoked streaky bacon, diced
Handful of roughly chopped fresh thyme leaves

1. Melt the butter in a large saucepan over a medium–low heat. Add the sliced leeks and cook gently for 10 minutes, stirring occasionally, until very soft. Add the fennel seeds and cook for 2–3 minutes. Stir in the chopped fennel and the potatoes.

2. Cover the vegetables with a sheet of wet baking paper and put a lid on the pan. Cook gently for 10–12 minutes, until the leeks are soft. Remove and discard the paper. Pour in the stock, bring to the boil, then cover and simmer for 30 minutes, until the vegetables are very tender.

3. Leave the soup to cool slightly, then pour half into a food processor or blender and whiz until smooth. Press the blended mixture through a sieve into the remaining soup in the pan. Stir in the cream and season to taste. Gently reheat the soup, but make sure it doesn't boil.

4. Meanwhile, make the winter greens and bacon. Discard the tough outer leaves of the cabbage. Roughly tear the remaining leaves, discarding any hard stalks, and blanch them in boiling salted water for 2–3 minutes. Refresh under cold running water and drain.

5. Melt the butter in a large frying pan over a medium heat. Add the pancetta or bacon, and cook for 3–4 minutes, until golden. Add the cabbage and thyme, and stir-fry for about 5 minutes, until the cabbage is tender. Season well.

6. Ladle the soup into deep bowls and spoon the winter greens and bacon into each bowl to serve.

MAGAZINE

delicious.

ONE-POT DISHES

Edited by Mitzie Wilson

Magazine Editor

Matthew Drennan

HarperCollins*Publishers*

Hearty Irish soup

This goes down a treat on a chilly evening. After a little preparation, the soup will happily simmer away while you're busy doing something else.

SERVES 4
READY IN ABOUT 2 HOURS

- 1 tbsp vegetable oil
- 2 tbsp butter
- 700g boneless lamb chump chops, trimmed and cut into small cubes
- 2 small onions, sliced
- 2 leeks, thickly sliced and washed thoroughly
- 2 large potatoes, cut into bite-sized chunks
- 1 carrot, thickly sliced
- ½ small swede, cut into bite-sized chunks
- Good sprig of fresh thyme, plus extra to garnish
- 2 tbsp chopped fresh parsley
- Irish soda bread or brown bread, to serve

1. Heat the oil and half the butter in a large saucepan over a medium–high heat. Add the cubes of lamb, in batches, and cook, turning occasionally, for 4–5 minutes, until well browned all over. Remove with a slotted spoon and set aside.

2. Add the onions to the pan and cook for 5 minutes, stirring often, until browned. Return the lamb to the pan and add the leeks. Pour in 1 litre of water and bring to the boil. Reduce the heat to low, cover and simmer gently for about 1 hour, stirring now and then.

3. Add the potatoes, carrot, swede and thyme, and continue cooking for a further 40 minutes, until the lamb is very tender. Remove from the heat and leave to stand for 5 minutes to allow the fat to settle on the surface of the soup.

4. Use a large spoon or ladle to skim off and discard the fat. Gradually whisk in the remaining butter. Stir in the parsley and season well with salt and pepper, then pour the liquid back over the lamb and vegetables.

5. To serve, ladle the soup into 4 warmed bowls and garnish with sprigs of fresh thyme. Eat with slices of Irish soda bread or brown bread.

Mulligatawny soup

This fab low-cal soup has many variations, and it's the perfect dish to freeze ahead. Ours is made with beef, but it's also great with leftover chicken or turkey.

SERVES 4
TAKES 50 MINUTES, PLUS FREEZING, DEFROSTING AND REHEATING

2 tbsp olive oil
350g rump steak, cut into pieces
Knob of butter
1 large onion, finely chopped
2 celery sticks, finely chopped
1 red pepper, seeded and chopped
3 garlic cloves, crushed
1 tbsp madras curry paste
400g creamed tomatoes or passata
600ml good beef stock, hot
100g freshly cooked basmati rice
1 apple, peeled, cored and grated
1 tbsp mango chutney
Fresh coriander leaves and natural yogurt, to garnish

1. Heat 1 tablespoon oil in a heavy-based saucepan and brown the steak over a high heat for 1 minute. Remove and set aside. Heat the remaining oil and the butter in the pan. Stir in the onion, celery and red pepper, and cook for 8 minutes. Add the garlic and curry paste, and cook for a further minute.

2. Return the steak to the pan, then pour over the tomatoes and stock. Bring to the boil and simmer for 20–25 minutes, until the beef is tender. Add the rice, apple and chutney, and simmer for 3 minutes.

3. Serve immediately or cool and put into food bags. Freeze for up to 3 months. Defrost and reheat for 10–12 minutes, until piping hot. Garnish with fresh coriander and natural yogurt.

Variation For a hearty vegetarian meal, leave out the beef and beef stock, add some red lentils or split peas and use vegetable stock.

Spiced beef and beet goulash soup

Don't be put off by the length of time this soup-cum-stew takes to cook; make a batch, eat some, and freeze the rest so you have a hearty supper at your fingertips when you fancy a night off from cooking.

SERVES 6–8
TAKES ABOUT 2 HOURS, 40 MINUTES IN THE OVEN, PLUS FREEZING, DEFROSTING AND REHEATING

2 tbsp olive oil
1kg beef chuck steak, cut into small cubes
2 large onions, finely chopped
4 garlic cloves, finely chopped
2 tbsp hot paprika
2 tsp cumin seeds
500g potatoes, cut into small cubes
2 x 400g cans chopped tomatoes
1½ litres beef stock
4 medium beetroot, scrubbed and trimmed
2 tbsp chopped fresh dill and 4 tbsp chopped fresh flatleaf parsley, to garnish
Soured cream, toasted sourdough or rye bread and Jarlsberg cheese, to serve

1. Preheat the oven to 200°C/fan 180°C/gas 6. Heat the oil in a large flameproof casserole and brown the beef all over, in 2 batches. Remove from the pan with a slotted spoon and set aside.

2. Add the chopped onions to the pan with the garlic and cook over a gentle heat for 3–4 minutes. Stir in the hot paprika and cumin seeds, and cook for a further minute. Add the potatoes, toss well with the onions and spices, then tip in the beef, chopped tomatoes and beef stock. Season well, cover and cook over a very gentle heat for 1½ hours or until the beef is tender and the sauce has thickened and reduced.

3. Meanwhile, wrap the beetroot in foil and bake for 40 minutes or until very tender. Remove the foil, leave to cool, then peel the beetroot and cut into 1cm pieces.

4. When the beef is cooked and tender, stir in the beetroot and remove from the heat. Leave to cool completely, then ladle into sturdy freezer bags or rigid containers and freeze for up to 2 months.

5. Defrost in the fridge overnight and reheat thoroughly. Stir in the herbs and ladle into bowls with a dollop of soured cream. Serve with some slices of toasted sourdough with melted Jarlsberg cheese on top.

Moroccan spiced soup with jewelled couscous

Harissa paste is a hot and spicy North African condiment based on a chilli paste. This recipe shows the spice at its best and is low in calories and fat, too.

SERVES 6
READY IN JUST OVER 1 HOUR

2 tbsp olive oil
450g beef rump or sirloin, trimmed of excess fat and cut into bite-sized pieces
2 small onions, chopped
2 garlic cloves, crushed
1 carrot, cut into small dice
2 celery sticks, diced
1 heaped tbsp harissa paste, plus extra to serve
2 tsp plain flour
1.2 litres vegetable stock, hot
400g can chopped tomatoes
75g ready-to-eat dried apricots
900g butternut squash, seeded, peeled and cut into small cubes

For the jewelled couscous
175g couscous
300ml vegetable stock, hot
2 tomatoes, seeded and diced
2 tbsp chopped fresh mint

1. Heat the olive oil in a heavy-based pan over a medium–high heat. Add the beef and cook for 5 minutes or until browned all over. Remove with a slotted spoon and set aside.

2. Add the onions and garlic to the pan, reduce the heat slightly and cook for 5 minutes, until softened. Add the carrot and celery, cover and cook for 5 minutes, until the vegetables have softened slightly. Stir in the harissa paste and flour, and cook for 2 minutes. Gradually whisk in the hot vegetable stock.

3. Stir in the tomatoes and apricots, then bring to the boil. Cover and simmer gently for 20 minutes. Season well with salt and pepper.

4. Add the butternut squash and return the beef to the soup. Cover and cook for about 25 minutes, stirring occasionally, until both the squash and beef are tender.

5. Meanwhile, make the jewelled couscous. Put the couscous in a large bowl. Pour over the hot stock, cover, and leave to stand for 5 minutes to absorb the liquid. Fluff up the grains with a fork, then stir in the tomatoes and mint. Season.

6. To serve, ladle the soup into warmed bowls. Pile a spoonful of couscous in the centre and serve with extra harissa on the side.

Prawn and Parmesan risotto soup

This creamy dish combines all that's soothing about soups with the satisfaction of a risotto.

SERVES 4
READY IN ABOUT 40 MINUTES

4 tbsp olive oil
4 large fresh sage leaves
25g butter
2 onions, finely chopped
1 small celery stick, finely sliced
300g risotto or arborio rice
1.2 litres chicken stock, hot
500g large raw peeled prawns
2 tbsp double cream
115g Parmesan, grated, plus shavings to serve

1. Heat half the oil in a frying pan over a medium heat. When hot, fry the sage leaves for a few seconds, until crisp. Remove with a slotted spoon and set aside on kitchen paper to drain.

2. Heat the butter and the remaining olive oil in the frying pan over a medium heat. Add the onions and celery, and cook, stirring occasionally, for 5 minutes, until softened. Add the risotto rice and cook for 1–2 minutes, stirring, until the grains are slightly translucent.

3. Add a ladleful of hot chicken stock to the pan. Cook, stirring, until the stock has been absorbed, then add another ladleful of stock. Continue adding the stock in this way until the rice is al dente but the liquid is soup-like – about 20 minutes.

4. Stir the prawns into the risotto soup and cook for 1–2 minutes, until pink and cooked through.

5. Stir the cream and grated Parmesan into the soup, then season with freshly ground black pepper.

6. To serve, divide the soup among 4 bowls. Garnish each one with a fried sage leaf and some Parmesan shavings.

Pasta and chickpea soup

A filling vegetable soup that freezes well, giving you a hearty meal to fall back on when time is too tight to cook.

SERVES 6–8
TAKES 50 MINUTES, PLUS FREEZING, DEFROSTING AND REHEATING

300g small macaroni pasta
2 tbsp extra-virgin olive oil, plus extra for the pasta
2 onions, finely chopped
3 garlic cloves, finely chopped
1 large fresh rosemary sprig, finely chopped, plus extra to garnish
1 tsp chilli flakes
2 x 400g cans chopped tomatoes
1 litre vegetable or chicken stock, hot
2 x 400g cans chickpeas, drained
2 tbsp balsamic vinegar
Parmesan shavings, to serve

1. Bring a pan of water to the boil and cook the macaroni for 2 minutes less than the packet instructions. Drain, toss in a little oil (to stop it sticking) and set aside. Heat 2 tablespoons of oil in the pan and gently cook the onions and garlic over a medium heat for 4–5 minutes. Stir in the rosemary and chilli flakes, and cook for a further 2 minutes.

2. Tip in the tomatoes, stock, chickpeas and a pinch of salt and a grinding of black pepper. Simmer gently for 20 minutes until thickened.

3. Stir in the vinegar and pasta, then remove from the heat. Cool completely, then ladle into freezer bags or containers. Freeze for up to 2 months.

4. Defrost overnight, then reheat on the hob and simmer for 2–3 minutes. Add a little boiling water if necessary, to loosen the soup. Serve with Parmesan shavings and garnish with little sprigs of rosemary.

Chicken noodle soup

This chicken noodle soup is in our Top 10 of comfort foods. Because it can be frozen, it's a meal-in-one that you can take out of the freezer and consume in no time.

SERVES 6
READY IN 2 HOURS

1.5kg whole chicken
4 carrots
3 celery sticks
3 onions
2 bay leaves
1 tbsp vegetable oil
1 leek, sliced
1 garlic clove, chopped
100g dried egg noodles
2cm piece fresh root ginger, grated
Chopped fresh parsley leaves and spring onions, to serve

1. Put the chicken in a large pan with 2 carrots and 2 celery sticks, all roughly chopped, 2 onions, quartered, and the bay leaves. Add about 2.5 litres of water – enough to cover the chicken and veg. Bring to the boil, skim off any fat and simmer for 1 hour. Remove the chicken and strain the stock into a large bowl, discarding the solids.

2. Heat the oil in the same pan over a medium heat. Add the leek, garlic and remaining carrots, cut into cubes, and the remaining onion and celery stick, both finely chopped. Cook for 5 minutes, until tender. Add 2 litres of the strained broth and bring to the boil, then reduce the heat to low and simmer gently for 10 minutes.

3. Meanwhile, remove the skin and strip the meat from the chicken. Tear the meat into bite-sized pieces and add to the soup. Add the noodles and ginger, and simmer for 4–5 minutes, until the noodles are tender. Season and garnish with the parsley and spring onions.

★ DELICIOUS. TIP To freeze, add the torn chicken but not the noodles or ginger. Remove from the heat and cool completely. Ladle into sturdy freezer bags or rigid containers and freeze for up to 2 months. Defrost, then reheat until piping hot. Add the noodles and ginger, and simmer for 4–5 minutes, until the noodles are tender. Season and garnish with the parsley and spring onions.

Spicy lentil and bacon soup

A tasty, chunky soup that can be frozen to make an ideal lunch or light supper that's to hand when you don't feel like cooking.

SERVES 6
READY IN 50 MINUTES

8 thick rashers smoked bacon, roughly chopped
2 tbsp olive oil
2 large leeks, cut into large chunks
4 garlic cloves, finely chopped
2 tsp chilli flakes
400g red lentils, rinsed
1½ litres vegetable stock, hot
400g can coconut milk
Juice of 1 lime
Fresh coriander leaves and 1 fresh chilli, sliced into thin strips, to garnish
Lime wedges, to serve

1. Heat a large pan and cook the bacon until golden. Remove with a slotted spoon and set aside. Heat the oil in the pan and gently cook the leeks and garlic for a few minutes until softened. Stir in the chilli and lentils, and toss together well for a few minutes.

2. Pour in the stock and coconut milk, and simmer for 15 minutes or until the lentils are cooked. Remove from the heat and stir in the bacon and the lime juice. Garnish with the fresh coriander and chilli and serve with lime wedges.

★ DELICIOUS. TIP To freeze: ladle into freezer bags or containers and freeze for up to 2 months. Defrost, then reheat thoroughly – add a splash of boiling water to loosen the mixture.

meat

Lamb and date tagine with pomegranate couscous

A delicously spicy one-pot that can simmer away for hours while you get on with something else.

SERVES 6–8
READY IN ABOUT 3½ HOURS

2 tbsp olive oil
2 onions, chopped
Large knob of fresh root ginger, chopped
4 garlic cloves, crushed
1 cinnamon stick
1 tbsp coriander seeds, crushed
1 tsp cumin seeds, lightly crushed
1.5kg boned shoulder or leg of lamb, cut into cubes
200g medjool dates, pitted
400g can chopped tomatoes
400ml lamb or chicken stock, hot
1 lemon and 1 lime, cut into wedges, to serve

For the pomegranate couscous
500g couscous
1 tbsp olive oil
Grated zest and juice of 1 lemon
Handful of fresh mint, roughly chopped
Seeds of 1 pomegranate

1. Heat the oil in a large, heavy-based pan and gently cook the onions, ginger and garlic for 10 minutes, until softened. Add all the spices and cook for 5 minutes, then add the lamb and cook for a further 10 minutes.

2. Add the dates, tomatoes and stock. Bring to the boil, then cover and simmer gently for 2½–3 hours, until the lamb is very tender.

3. Place the couscous, oil and lemon zest and juice in a bowl, and cover with 600ml boiling water. Cover and leave to cool completely, then use a fork to fluff up the couscous and stir in the mint and pomegranate seeds.

4. Serve the couscous with the tagine and garnish with citrus wedges.

Lancashire hotpot

A welcome and warming winter dish, this is a real English favourite that's like a Sunday lunch all in one pot.

SERVES 4
TAKES 30 MINUTES, PLUS 50 MINUTES IN THE OVEN

1 tbsp olive oil
500g lamb leg steaks, cubed
2 tbsp seasoned plain flour
1 large onion, sliced
2 small carrots, sliced
300ml chicken stock, hot
1 tbsp Worcestershire sauce
A few fresh thyme sprigs
600g waxy potatoes
Butter

1. Preheat the oven to 190°C/fan 170°C/gas 5. Heat the olive oil in a large, wide pan over a medium heat. Dust the lamb steaks in the flour and fry, in batches ina wide, shallow hob and ovenproof pan, until browned. Set aside.

2. Add the onion to the pan with the carrots and cook for 5 minutes. Return the lamb to the pan with the stock, Worcestershire sauce and thyme. Season, remove from the heat and tip into a bowl.

3. Thinly slice the potatoes and place half in an overlapping layer in the pan. Top with the meat mixture, then layer over the remaining potato and dot with butter. Cover and cook in the oven for 30 minutes, then remove the lid and cook for a further 20 minutes, until the potatoes are golden brown.

Braised lamb shanks with lemon, garlic and parsley

A gastropub favourite, lamb shanks love being left to cook until succulent and intensely savoury. Even better made in advance and chilled overnight.

SERVES 4
TAKES ABOUT 30 MINUTES, PLUS ABOUT 3 HOURS IN THE OVEN

- 2 tbsp olive oil
- 4 x 400g lamb shanks
- 1 small onion, chopped
- 1 small fennel bulb, chopped
- 3 fresh bay leaves, torn
- 2 fresh rosemary sprigs
- 5 garlic cloves, 4 chopped, 1 whole
- 8 fresh thyme sprigs
- 700ml lamb, chicken or beef stock, hot
- 150ml white wine
- Finely grated zest of 1 lemon
- 2 tbsp finely chopped fresh parsley
- 2 tbsp extra-virgin olive oil

Variation Replace the lamb shanks with generous chunks of lamb shoulder; they may require a slightly shorter cooking time, but will be just as flavoursome.

1. Preheat the oven to 140°C/fan 120°C/gas 1. Heat the olive oil in a large, wide pan with a lid over a medium heat. Season the shanks and brown all over in the pan for 8–10 minutes. Remove to a plate. Add the onion and fennel to the pan and cook for 8 minutes, stirring, until turning golden. Add the bay leaves, rosemary, chopped garlic and half the thyme, and return the shanks to the pan.

2. Pour in the stock and wine, and heat until just bubbling. Cover with a tight-fitting lid and bake for 2½–3 hours, until the meat is meltingly tender.

3. Meanwhile, crush the remaining garlic with a pinch of salt and finely chop the remaining thyme. Put in a bowl with the lemon zest, parsley and extra-virgin olive oil and mix together well. Season with black pepper only.

4. Transfer the shanks to a dish and cover loosely with foil. Skim off and discard the fat from the surface of the sauce, then bring to the boil and simmer for a few minutes. Mix 2 tablespoons sauce into the lemon, garlic and parsley mixture.

5. Divide the lamb shanks among the plates. Strain over the sauce and lemon, garlic and parsley mixture and serve with mashed potato.

★ DELICIOUS. TIP To freeze: freeze at the end of step 2. Thaw, reheat on the hob thoroughly and complete the recipe.

Lamb biryani

The biryani – baked rice usually layered with meat – first originated in the Moghul cuisine of the 16th–19th century. It was a festive dish, costly to prepare and eaten mainly in the royal courts.

SERVES 6
TAKES 55 MINUTES, 30–35 MINUTES IN THE OVEN, PLUS OVERNIGHT MARINATING

250ml natural yogurt, plus extra to serve
1 green chilli, seeded and finely sliced
4 garlic cloves, crushed
50g fresh root ginger, grated
½ tsp each ground cloves and ground cinnamon
2 tsp each ground cumin and ground coriander
750g lamb leg steaks, trimmed of excess fat and cut into bite-sized pieces
350g basmati rice
100ml milk
1 tsp ground saffron
2 large onions, finely sliced
75g ghee, plus extra 1 tbsp
1 long cinnamon stick, broken into 3 pieces
12 cardamom pods, cracked
Crispy onions and chopped fresh coriander, to garnish

1. Mix the yogurt, chilli, garlic, ginger, cloves, cinnamon, half the ground cumin and coriander, lamb and seasoning. Cover and chill overnight.

2. The next day, remove the lamb from the fridge. Rinse the rice and soak in cold water for 30 minutes. Heat the milk and stir in the saffron.

3. Meanwhile, preheat the oven to 150°C/fan 130°C/gas 2. In a wide pan, cook the onions in the 75g ghee over a medium heat for 15 minutes, until golden. Stir in the remaining cumin and coriander, and cook for 1 minute, then set aside.

4. Drain the rice. Bring some water, the cinnamon stick, cardamom pods and a pinch of salt to the boil in a pan. Add the rice, stir and boil for 2 minutes, drain and mix into the onions.

5. Melt 1 tablespoon ghee in a flameproof casserole with a tight-fitting lid over a low heat. Spoon in one-third of the rice, then top with half the lamb. Repeat, drizzling with half the saffron milk. Cover with the remaining rice and saffron milk. Cover with foil and a lid, heat for 30 seconds, then bake for 30–35 minutes, until the lamb is tender. Serve sprinkled with crispy onions and coriander.

★ DELICIOUS. TIP To make the crispy onions, slice 1 large onion and put in a bowl with 25g ghee. Cover with cling film, pierce once and microwave on high for 15–16 minutes, shaking towards the end of cooking until the onions are crisp and golden.

Variation Instead of lamb, use lean chicken pieces or tender beef steaks, such as sirloin, cut into bite-sized pieces.

Summery braised shoulder of lamb

Anchovies and lamb might seem like an unusual pairing, but the flavours work well together in this summery roast.

SERVES 4
READY IN ABOUT 2½ HOURS

1.5kg bone-in shoulder of lamb
6 garlic cloves, roughly chopped
6 anchovy fillets in olive oil, drained and roughly chopped
Leaves from 2 fresh rosemary sprigs, roughly chopped
2 red chillies, seeded and diced (optional)
1 tbsp light olive oil
2 red onions, halved and sliced
200ml white wine
400g can whole plum tomatoes
2 tbsp Worcestershire sauce
½ tsp sugar
Large handful of fresh flatleaf parsley, to garnish
Rice or flatbread, to serve

1. Season the lamb well and set aside. Mix the garlic, anchovies, rosemary and chillies (if using) in a bowl. Set aside.

2. Heat the oil over a medium heat in a large flameproof casserole. Brown the lamb, fat-side down first, for 10 minutes, turning occasionally, until golden all over. Remove to a plate.

3. Add the garlic and anchovy mixture to the casserole and cook for 1–2 minutes. Stir in the onions and cook for 6–8 minutes, to soften, then add the wine.

4. Squish the tomatoes in a colander over a bowl so you are left with a pulp. Add this to the casserole with the Worcestershire sauce and sugar.

5. Return the lamb to the pan and add enough water just to cover. Cover and simmer for 2 hours, or until you can nudge the meat from the bone with the back of a spoon.

6. If the dish seems too brothy, remove the lid and turn up the heat to reduce the juices. Season, scatter with parsley and serve with rice or, if you prefer, flatbread.

Pot-roasted leg of lamb with redcurrant jelly and mint

This is so simple to prepare and makes an ideal Sunday lunch that can be cooking while you go for a long walk to be meltingly tender on your return.

SERVES 8
TAKES 15 MINUTES, PLUS 6 HOURS IN THE OVEN

2 tbsp good-quality olive oil
2kg leg of lamb
4 red onions, quartered
225ml red wine
4 tbsp redcurrant jelly
2 tbsp balsamic vinegar
2 tbsp chopped fresh mint
1 tbsp chopped fresh sage

1. Preheat the oven to 110°C/fan 90°C/gas ¼. Warm the olive oil in a large casserole over a medium heat. Season the lamb, add to the casserole and brown on all sides for about 10 minutes.

2. Add the onions, red wine, redcurrant jelly, vinegar, mint and sage. Bring to the boil, then cover tightly with a lid and place in the oven. Roast for about 6 hours until the meat is succulent and tender.

Lamb and apricots

This fragrant, sweet-and-sour casserole is inspired by the tagines of north Africa.

SERVES 4
READY IN 2 HOURS 35 MINUTES

1 cinnamon stick
3 cloves
1kg diced shoulder or neck of lamb, trimmed of any excess fat
1½ tbsp mild olive oil
1 onion, roughly chopped
2 celery sticks, roughly chopped
2 leeks, washed and roughly chopped
3 garlic cloves, roughly chopped
2 bay leaves
3 tbsp red or white wine vinegar
1 tbsp tomato purée
350ml chicken or vegetable stock, hot
500g fresh apricots, halved and stoned or 410g can apricot halves in fruit juice, drained
4 tbsp natural yogurt (strained Greek-style is best)

1. Dry-fry the whole spices in a large, heavy-based pan or casserole over a high heat for no more than a minute. Tip out and set aside.

2. Season the lamb well. Heat the oil in the pan or casserole over a high heat. Add half the lamb and brown on all sides. Remove with a slotted spoon and set aside while you brown the remaining lamb, then set aside as well.

3. Add the chopped vegetables and garlic to the pan, and cook gently, stirring occasionally, for 15 minutes, until tender. Don't let them brown.

4. Stir the toasted spices into the cooked vegetables, then add the bay leaves, vinegar and tomato purée. Return the meat to the pan and stir. Add just enough stock to cover the meat. Bring to a simmer, then cover and cook over a low heat for 1 hour.

5. Add the apricots, but don't stir them into the stew. Re-cover the pan and cook for another hour. Keep checking to make sure the stock has not reduced too much – top up if needs be.

6. Once the lamb is tender (you should be able to cut the pieces with a spoon), remove the pan from the heat. Check the seasoning, then gently stir the apricots into the stew. You can either divide among bowls and garnish each portion with a tablespoon of yogurt, or serve the yogurt on the side.

Easy lamb tagine

This quick and simple recipe uses lots of storecupboard spices to create a satisfying supper that works all year round.

SERVES 4
TAKES 10 MINUTES, PLUS
50 MINUTES–1 HOUR COOKING

400g lamb leg steaks, cubed
2 tbsp olive oil
1 onion, sliced
2 garlic cloves, chopped
2 tsp ground coriander
2 tsp ground cumin
1 tsp ground ginger
Pinch of ground cinnamon
400g can chopped tomatoes
200ml chicken stock, hot
100g pitted prunes, chopped
1 tbsp ground almonds
Handful of chopped fresh coriander
Herby couscous, to serve

1. Brown the lamb in the oil in a pan. Set aside. Add the onion and garlic, and fry for 5 minutes.

2. Add the ground coriander, cumin, ginger and cinnamon, and fry for 2 minutes.

3. Return the lamb to the pan with the tomatoes and stock. Add the pitted prunes. Simmer for 40–45 minutes.

4. Stir in the ground almonds and fresh coriander. Serve with herby couscous.

Quick lamb, orange and fennel spring stew

This quick stew makes a light yet filling one-pot family supper.

SERVES 4
READY IN 45 MINUTES

600g cubed lamb (see tip)
2 tbsp seasoned plain flour
2 tbsp olive oil
1 red onion, thinly sliced
2 garlic cloves, chopped
1 tsp fennel seeds
Grated zest and juice of 2 oranges
300ml fresh chicken stock, hot
500g baby new potatoes
1 large fennel bulb, roughly chopped
1 tbsp red wine vinegar
2 tbsp chopped fresh parsley
Steamed spinach or spring greens, to serve

1. In a bowl, coat the lamb in the seasoned flour. Heat the oil in a large frying pan over a high heat. Add the lamb, in batches, and brown for 5 minutes. Remove and set aside.

2. Add the onion, garlic and fennel seeds to the pan, and cook for 5 minutes, stirring occasionally, until softened and golden.

3. Stir in the orange zest and juice, the chicken stock, potatoes, fennel and browned lamb. Bring to the boil, then cover and simmer gently for 20 minutes or until the potatoes are tender.

4. Stir in the vinegar and parsley, and adjust the seasoning to taste. Serve in warmed bowls with steamed spinach or spring greens.

★ DELICIOUS. TIP Lamb is young and always tender, which is why this stew can be cooked so quickly. Use ready-cubed lamb or choose a cut of lamb you prefer and chop it up – for lean meat, choose leg; if you like it slightly fattier, try neck fillet.

Variation Omit the fennel seeds and fresh fennel and add 250g frozen broad beans to the casserole for the last 5 minutes of cooking. Stir in a little chopped mint just before serving.

Moussaka

Moussaka is a quintessential Greek dish made using local ingredients such as lamb, aubergines, oregano, olive oil and feta. This classic recipe is topped with a bubbling mixture of Greek yogurt and two cheeses.

SERVES 4
TAKES 50 MINUTES, PLUS 35 MINUTES IN THE OVEN

1 tbsp olive oil, plus extra for brushing
1 large onion, finely chopped
2 garlic cloves, crushed
500g lamb mince
1 tbsp tomato purée
½ tsp ground cinnamon
400g can chopped tomatoes
2 tsp dried oregano
600g (about 2 medium) aubergines

For the topping
150ml Greek yogurt
1 medium egg, beaten
25g freshly grated Parmesan
50g feta

1. Heat the oil in a large frying pan over a medium heat. Add the onion and garlic, and cook, stirring, for 5 minutes, until soft. Increase the heat, add the lamb and cook, stirring, for 5 minutes, until browned. Drain off the fat through a sieve, then return the meat to the pan.

2. Add the purée and cinnamon, and cook, stirring, for 1 minute. Add the tomatoes, then half-fill the can with water and pour into the pan. Add the oregano, season, and bring to the boil. Reduce the heat and simmer, stirring occasionally, for 20 minutes.

3. Meanwhile, preheat the grill to medium–high. Cut each aubergine diagonally into 5mm-thick slices. Brush with oil, put half on a baking sheet and grill for 5 minutes, turning halfway, until pale golden. Drain on kitchen paper while grilling the remainder.

4. Preheat the oven to 200°C/fan 180°C/gas 6. For the topping, mix together the yogurt, egg and half the cheeses. Season with pepper.

5. Spread half the lamb mixture in a deep 1.2-litre ovenproof dish. Overlap with half the aubergine and the rest of the lamb. Top with remaining aubergine, spoon over the yogurt mixture and scatter with the remaining cheeses. Bake for 35 minutes or until golden and bubbling.

Variation Instead of layering up the mince with aubergines, you can bake the aubergines until soft, scoop out the centres (leaving a 1cm rim), then chop the aubergine flesh into the mince. Fill the shells with the mince, sprinkle with cheese and bake until golden.

South African bobotie

Bobotie is a dish that has been known in the Cape of Good Hope since the 17th century. A spiced, minced meat dish with an egg-based topping, this popular recipe also features cinnamon, curry powder, apples and almonds.

SERVES 4
TAKES 50 MINUTES, PLUS
30 MINUTES IN THE OVEN

1 tbsp olive oil, plus extra for brushing
1 large onion, finely chopped
2 garlic cloves, crushed
500g lamb mince
1 tbsp tomato purée
½ tsp ground cinnamon
1½ tbsp medium curry powder
1 dessert apple, cored and chopped
40g ground almonds
25g raisins
2 tbsp fresh lemon juice
1 white bread slice soaked in 125ml milk

For the topping
300ml Greek yogurt
2 medium eggs, beaten
15g flaked almonds

1. Heat the oil in a large frying pan over a medium heat. Add the onion and garlic and cook, stirring, for 5 minutes, until soft. Increase the heat, add the lamb and cook, stirring, for 5 minutes, until browned. Drain off the fat in a sieve, then return the meat to the pan.

2. Preheat the oven to 200°C/fan 180°C/gas 6. Add the purée and cinnamon and cook, stirring, for 1 minute. Add the curry powder, apple, ground almonds, raisins, lemon juice and 250ml water. Simmer for 10 minutes, stir in the bread and milk, then tip into an ovenproof dish.

3. Mix the yogurt with the eggs, spoon over the mince and top with the flaked almonds. Bake for 30 minutes.

Curried lamb mince cobbler

Tantalise your tastebuds with luscious lamb and clouds of doughy cobbler. A real winter warmer.

SERVES 4
TAKES 50 MINUTES, PLUS
15–25 MINUTES IN THE OVEN

1 tbsp olive oil
1 large onion, finely chopped
1 tbsp mild or medium curry powder
500g lamb mince
450g swede, cubed
3 tbsp mango chutney, plus extra to serve
400ml fresh lamb stock, hot
Seasonal vegetables, to serve

For the cobbler
225g self-raising flour
60g butter, cut into cubes
1 tsp cumin seeds
1 medium egg
125ml milk

1. Heat the oil in a large, deep frying pan over a medium heat. Add the onion and cook for 5 minutes, stirring occasionally, until soft. Stir in the curry powder and cook for 1 minute. Increase the heat, add the mince and cook for 5 minutes, breaking it up with the spoon, until browned.

2. Stir in the swede, chutney and stock, and bring to a simmer. Cook for 20 minutes, stirring, until the swede is tender. Season and tip into 4 (about 500ml each) dishes or 1 deep 2-litre ovenproof dish.

3. Preheat the oven to 190°C/fan 170°C/gas 5. Make the cobbler. Sift the flour and a good pinch of salt into a bowl. Add the butter and rub in with your fingertips to coarse crumbs. Stir in the cumin. In a separate bowl, beat the egg with the milk, then add to the flour mixture and mix to a firm dough. Dot clumps over the mince, spaced apart.

4. Bake for 15–20 minutes for individual portions or 25 minutes for the large dish. Serve with extra chutney and seasonal vegetables.

Mutton, vegetable and barley stew

This lovely stew is based on the traditional Scotch broth ingredients of barley, swede and carrots.

SERVES 4
TAKES 25 MINUTES, PLUS
2½ HOURS IN THE OVEN

1kg boned shoulder or leg of mutton, cut into 2cm cubes
3 tbsp plain flour
2 tbsp olive oil
15g butter
2 celery sticks, roughly sliced
1 leek, washed and roughly sliced
2 garlic cloves, crushed
2 carrots, roughly sliced
400g floury potatoes, roughly diced
400g swede, roughly diced
500ml fresh lamb stock, hot
400ml carrot juice
2 fresh sprigs each rosemary and thyme, plus extra to garnish
100g pearl barley
Rustic bread, to serve

1. Preheat the oven to 180°C/fan 160°C/gas 4. Put the cubed mutton in a large bowl, add the flour and season. Toss well.

2. Put a large casserole over a high heat. Add the oil and brown the mutton in batches.

3. Turn the heat down to medium and add the butter. Stir in the celery, leek, garlic, carrots, potatoes and swede, and toss well. Cook, stirring occasionally, until browning a little. Pour in the lamb stock and carrot juice, then add the rosemary and thyme. Bring to the boil, cover and cook in the oven for 2½ hours, until tender.

4. Stir in the pearl barley 30 minutes before the end of the cooking time, so it absorbs the juices and becomes tender. The stew should be thick and juicy. Season, garnish with rosemary and thyme, and serve with rustic bread.

Mediterranean beef pots

Cottage pie with a Mediterranean makeover; you can easily double this recipe to make a fantastic family meal, too.

SERVES 2
READY IN 40 MINUTES

1 tbsp olive oil
100g ready-diced onions or 1 small onion, diced
250g lean beef mince
1 tbsp tomato purée
230g can chopped tomatoes
Fresh oregano leaves (from a bunch), plus extra to garnish
Handful of chargrilled peppers (from a jar)
Handful of pitted black olives
Ready-grilled aubergines (from a jar)
100ml Greek yogurt
1 medium free-range egg
50g feta, crumbled

1. In a large frying pan, heat the olive oil and cook the onions until softened. Add the beef mince, season, break up with a spoon and fry until browned. Stir through the tomato purée and pour over the tomatoes, some fresh oregano leaves and a splash of water. Bring to a simmer and bubble rapidly for 15 minutes.

2. Preheat the grill to medium–high. Stir through the chargrilled peppers and the olives, then divide between 2 x 350ml ovenproof dishes. Top each with a layer of aubergine slices.

3. In a bowl, mix the Greek yogurt with the egg and spoon it over the aubergines. Scatter with feta. Pop under the grill for 5 minutes until browned.

4. Serve scattered with more oregano leaves.

Pork and pepper goulash

Turn pork chops into something a bit special for a tasty midweek meal to serve with mash and a green vegetable.

SERVES 4
READY IN 40 MINUTES

2 tbsp olive oil
1 red onion, sliced
1 tbsp sweet smoked paprika
1 tsp caraway seeds (optional)
700g pork chops, trimmed of excess fat and cut into pieces
400g can chopped tomatoes
300g jar roasted red peppers, sliced
Handful of chopped fresh parsley
Soured cream, to serve (optional)
Mashed potato, to serve (optional)

1. Heat the oil in a pan and gently fry the onion for 5 minutes, until tender. Add the paprika and caraway, if using, and stir for 1 minute.

2. Brown the pork in the pan for 5 minutes, then add the tomatoes and simmer for 15 minutes. Add the peppers and cook for a further 5 minutes, until the pork is tender and cooked. Season well and stir through the parsley. Serve with a dollop of soured cream and some mashed potato, if you like,.

Variation Turn this into a veggie recipe by replacing the pork with some cubed courgettes and halved mushrooms in step 2. Then follow the recipe in the same way.

Pearl barley, bacon and leek casserole

Pearl barley is an underrated ingredient, but this recipe should put a stop to that. This is a rich, warming and delicious dish ideal for those times when you need to summon up extra energy.

SERVES 4
READY IN 1 HOUR

75g butter, plus extra for frying
1 tbsp olive oil
250g piece bacon or pork belly, cut into chunks
2 leeks, thickly sliced
2 garlic cloves, crushed
300g pearl barley
300g butternut squash, peeled, seeded and cubed
3 tbsp fresh thyme leaves
1 litre chicken stock
175g self-raising flour
75g Cheddar, grated
2 tbsp chopped fresh flatleaf parsley

1. Heat a large pan over a medium heat. Add a good knob of butter and the olive oil, and fry the bacon or pork belly for 5 minutes, until golden.

2. Add the leeks and garlic, fry for a few minutes.

3. Add the pearl barley, butternut squash, thyme and chicken stock. Season. Simmer for 25 minutes, until the barley is nearly tender.

4. Meanwhile, make the dumplings. In a bowl, mix the flour with the butter, Cheddar, chopped parsley, some seasoning and a splash of water until it forms a soft dough. Roll into walnut-sized dumplings, add to the casserole and cook for a further 10–15 minutes. Serve immediately.

★ DELICIOUS. TIP Pearl barley is really versatile, so don't just use it for stews and casseroles – use it instead of risotto rice or even just cooked in stock and cooled then stirred into salads.

Braised gammon and quick Boston beans

Although it takes a little while to cook, this is a very easy family-friendly recipe and it's worth the wait while the gammon braises in the oven.

SERVES 4

TAKES 25 MINUTES, PLUS 50 MINUTES TO BRAISE, PLUS SOAKING (IF NEEDED)

- 1 small (about 850g) smoked gammon joint
- 1 onion, finely chopped
- 1 garlic clove, crushed
- 2 tsp tomato purée
- 2 tbsp maple syrup
- 1 tbsp molasses or dark brown sugar
- 2 tsp English mustard powder
- ½ tsp ground cinnamon
- 2 x 400g cans cannellini or haricot beans, drained and rinsed
- 300ml chicken or vegetable stock, hot
- Steamed buttered greens, to serve

1. Preheat the oven to 180°C/fan 160°C/ gas 4. Soak the gammon in cold water, if necessary (see tip, below) and rinse well. Pat dry with kitchen paper and set aside.

2. Heat a roasting tin or casserole over a medium heat and brown the gammon, skin-side down at first, until golden all over – about 5–6 minutes. Set aside. Add the onion to the tin, stir for 1 minute, then add the garlic, tomato purée, maple syrup, molasses or sugar, mustard and cinnamon. Cook for a further minute, then add the beans and stock. Cover with a lid or foil and bake for 10 minutes. Add the gammon, re-cover and bake in the oven for a further 40 minutes. Cook uncovered for the last 10 minutes to reduce the liquid slightly.

3. Season with black pepper, thickly slice the gammon and serve with the beans and some steamed buttered greens.

★ DELICIOUS. TIP Smoked gammon can sometimes be overly salty, so give it a quick soak in cold water for 15 minutes before using. If you buy gammon from a butcher, check whether it has been pre-soaked – if it has, you can skip the soaking step.

Oven-baked sausages and balsamic tomatoes

A homely, warming meal of sausages and tomatoes that will satisfy the largest of appetites.

SERVES 4
TAKES 5 MINUTES, PLUS 30 MINUTES IN THE OVEN

12 sausages
6 garlic cloves, sliced
2 red onions, cut into wedges
Olive oil
600g cherry tomatoes, halved
3 tbsp balsamic vinegar
Handful of torn fresh basil leaves

1. In a large roasting tin, toss together the sausages, garlic and red onions with a little olive oil.

2. Roast in a preheated oven at 200°C/fan 180°C/gas 6 for 20 minutes, until golden.

3. Add the cherry tomatoes and balsamic vinegar. Season and toss together gently.

4. Return to the oven for a further 10 minutes, stir in the basil leaves and serve.

Potato and sauerkraut gratin

Here the sauerkraut adds a Germanic feel to a potato recipe that's good served hot or cold.

SERVES 4
TAKES 30 MINUTES, PLUS ABOUT 50 MINUTES IN THE OVEN

1 tbsp butter, lard or duck fat
200g smoked streaky bacon, diced
2 onions, sliced
1 tsp juniper berries, crushed
1 tsp green peppercorns, crushed
1 bay leaf
3 tbsp sauerkraut (from a jar)
6 medium waxy potatoes
100ml white wine or cider
200ml light vegetable stock or water, hot
3 tbsp crème fraîche

1. Heat the butter, lard or fat in a frying pan and, when it is fizzing, add the bacon. Fry for a few minutes, then add the onions, spices and bay leaf. Cover and sweat for 7–8 minutes, stirring halfway, until the onions are soft. Fold in the sauerkraut.

2. Meanwhile, cut the potatoes into 5mm-thick slices. Blanch in salted boiling water for about 5 minutes, then drain well and set aside.

3. Preheat the oven to 190°C/fan 170°C/gas 5. Add the wine or cider to the onion mixture and bubble for 2–3 minutes. Add the stock and simmer rapidly for 6–8 minutes, stirring occasionally, until three-quarters of the liquid has evaporated. Take off the heat and stir in the crème fraîche.

4. Fill a deep 2-litre ovenproof dish with alternate layers of potatoes and the onion mixture, pouring over any juices left from the onion mixture. Cover with foil and bake for about 50 minutes or until very tender.

★ DELICIOUS. TIP Eat hot or cold, either on its own or with smoked salmon or leftover meat cold cuts.

Winter greens risotto with crunchy bacon

Enjoy your winter greens with this tasty credit-crunch dish.

SERVES 4
READY IN ABOUT 30 MINUTES

2 tbsp olive oil
150g streaky bacon, sliced
200g winter greens, shredded
Knob of butter
2 large shallots, finely sliced
350g risotto rice
250ml white wine
750ml–1 litre chicken stock, hot
35g Parmesan or
Grana Padano, grated

1. Heat half the olive oil in a frying pan and fry the bacon until just crisp. Add the winter greens and stir-fry for 5 minutes, until wilted. Tip into a bowl and set aside.

2. Heat the butter and remaining olive oil in the pan, and gently fry the shallots for 5 minutes, until soft.

3. Add the risotto rice and cook for a few minutes. Add the white wine and stir until absorbed. Gradually add the hot stock, a ladleful at a time, stirring until absorbed.

4. When the risotto is al dente – after about 20 minutes – stir in the bacon and greens, Parmesan or Grana Padano, and season.

★ DELICIOUS. TIP Winter greens is a generic term that covers green-leafed veg that are at their best at this time of year. Use any of the following: Savoy cabbage, curly kale, cavolo nero and Swiss chard.

Pork and butter bean stew

A filling and warming stew that's ideal for a cold winter's night.

SERVES 4
READY IN 50 MINUTES

150g chorizo, diced
1 red onion, finely sliced
2 garlic cloves, crushed
Drizzle of vegetable oil
2 large or 4 small pork chops, trimmed of excess fat and cut into pieces
400g can chopped tomatoes
100ml chicken stock
A few fresh thyme sprigs
400g can butter beans, drained and rinsed

1. Heat a casserole, add the chorizo and dry-fry over a medium heat for 5 minutes, until crisp. Add the onion and garlic, and fry for 5 minutes, until tender. Remove from the pan and set aside.

2. Heat a drizzle of vegetable oil in the casserole and fry the pork until browned all over.

3. Return the chorizo and onion mixture to the casserole, and add the tomatoes, chicken stock and thyme. Season well, bring to the boil and simmer for 15 minutes.

4. Add the butter beans and cook for a further 5–10 minutes. Check the seasoning and serve with baked potatoes.

Variation For a different twist, swap the chopped tomatoes for cider or apple juice and add 75ml double cream at the end.

Sausage, chicken liver and porcini mushroom cannelloni

A perfect prepare-ahead dish that will satisfy the hungriest of appetites at short notice.

SERVES 4
TAKES 50 MINUTES, PLUS
30 MINUTES IN THE OVEN

15g dried porcini mushrooms
2 tbsp extra-virgin olive oil
1 small onion, finely chopped
2 garlic cloves, crushed
400g pack pork sausages
125g good-quality chicken livers, trimmed and finely chopped
2 tsp fresh thyme leaves
2 tbsp tomato purée
75ml chicken stock
150g (6 sheets) fresh egg lasagne
150g tub fresh tomato and mascarpone sauce
Butter, for greasing
25g Parmesan, finely grated
Fresh basil leaves, to garnish

1. Soak the mushrooms in 100ml hot water. Heat the oil in a large pan, add the onions and garlic, and cook gently for 10 minutes, until soft and lightly browned.

2. Meanwhile, skin the sausages and break the meat into small pieces. Preheat the oven to 200°C/fan 180°C/gas 6. Add to the pan and cook, breaking up the meat with a wooden spoon as it browns. Add the chicken livers and cook for 2–3 minutes. Drain the mushrooms, reserving the liquid, and chop finely. Add to the pan with the thyme and cook for 2 minutes. Stir in the tomato purée, reserved mushroom liquid and stock, and simmer for 5 minutes, until thickened.

3. Bring a large pan of salted water to the boil. Drop in the lasagne sheets, take the pan off the heat and leave to soak for 5 minutes. Drain, refresh under cold water, then separate the sheets.

4. Spoon a thin layer of the tomato and mascarpone sauce over the base of a buttered 20cm x 30cm ovenproof dish. Spoon the filling along 1 short edge of each lasagne sheet and roll up. Put on the sauce, seam-side down. Spoon over the remaining sauce and scatter with Parmesan. Bake for 30 minutes or until golden and bubbling. Serve scattered with basil leaves.

★ DELICIOUS. TIP To freeze: cool, then wrap in cling film. Freeze for up to 3 months. Thaw for 24 hours in the fridge, then bring up to room temperature before cooking as above.

Paprika pork with chickpeas

This spicy dish is deeply satisfying and packed with flavour.

SERVES 4
TAKES 15 MINUTES, PLUS
25 MINUTES IN THE OVEN

- 1 tbsp vegetable oil
- 4 x 175g pork loin steaks, seasoned
- 1 onion, finely sliced
- 2 tsp paprika
- 2 tbsp tomato purée
- 1 red pepper, seeded and diced
- 400g can plum tomatoes
- 1 large courgette, diced
- 410g can chickpeas, drained and rinsed
- Crusty bread or rice, to serve

1. Preheat the oven to 190°C/fan 170°C/gas 5. Heat the vegetable oil in a large roasting tin over a high heat. Add the pork and brown for 2 minutes each side. Lift the pork out and set aside.

2. Add the sliced onion to the tin and cook, stirring, for 5 minutes. Stir in the paprika and tomato purée for 1 minute, then add the remaining ingredients. Season, return the pork to the pan and cover tightly with foil.

3. Bake in the oven for 25 minutes or until the pork is cooked and the vegetables tender. Serve the pork with crusty fresh bread or rice.

Variation Vegetarians can leave out the pork and add 2 diced aubergines along with the onions.

Normandy pork with cider

The Dijon mustard and crème fraîche give this freeze-ahead French recipe a lovely creamy flavour and complement the pork perfectly.

SERVES 8
TAKES 1¾ HOURS, PLUS COOLING

4 tbsp vegetable oil
1kg lean pork, diced
2 large onions, diced
2 large carrots, thickly sliced
2 parsnips, thickly sliced
2 leeks, washed and sliced into 3cm lengths
500ml dry cider
2 bay leaves
1 tsp Dijon mustard
1 tbsp cornflour
200g half-fat crème fraîche
2 Cox's apples

1. Heat the oil in a casserole over a medium–high heat. Fry the pork in batches, until just browned. Remove with a slotted spoon and set aside in a bowl. Add the onions to the casserole and fry for 5 minutes, stirring, until just transparent. Return the pork to the casserole.

2. Add the vegetables to the casserole, then pour over the cider and add the bay leaves. Bring to the boil. Cover and simmer for 1 hour, or until the pork is tender.

3. Stir the mustard and cornflour into the crème fraîche, then stir into the casserole. Core and cut the apples into wedges. Add to the casserole and simmer for 5–8 minutes, or until the apples are tender and the sauce has thickened. Season and serve.

★ DELICIOUS. TIP To freeze: cook until the end of step 2. Allow to cool, then freeze in portions for up to 3 months. Thaw for 24 hours in the fridge. To reheat, put into a large pan over a medium heat until piping hot.

Braised beef winter stew

Pickled red cabbage would make a fantastic accompaniment to this inexpensive and comforting wintry stew for four.

SERVES 4
READY IN 3 HOURS

- 2 tbsp olive oil
- 1.6kg piece rolled and tied brisket, blade or braising steak
- 2 carrots, halved lengthways and cut into large chunks
- 2 celery sticks, chopped
- 2 onions, cut into small wedges
- 400g can chopped tomatoes
- 2 bay leaves
- 1 litre hot beef stock, made from 1 stock cube
- 250g dried country vegetable mixture, including split peas, lentils and pearl barley
- Small handful of fresh flatleaf parsley, finely chopped

1. Heat the oil in a large casserole and sear the beef all over until just browned. Add all of the vegetables and bay leaves to the pan and cover with the stock. Bring to the boil, then cover and reduce the heat and simmer gently for 1 hour.
2. Add the dried pulses and continue to cook for a further 1½ hours, until the stock is thickened and the pulses are cooked. Remove the beef and cut into thick slices, discarding the string.
3. Ladle the stock and pulses into bowls and serve with the beef slices and a good sprinkling of chopped parsley.

Variation For a vegetarian version, omit the beef, and cook the pulses and veg in vegetable stock. Serve with a nut roast.

Mexican minced beef and spicy polenta cobbler

A fantastic, Mexican-inspired take on an old favourite, this is a fail-safe dish for easy entertaining.

SERVES 8
TAKES 1 HOUR, PLUS 20 MINUTES IN THE OVEN

4 tbsp sunflower oil
3 medium onions, finely chopped
4 garlic cloves, crushed
1 tsp crushed dried chillies
2 tsp freshly ground cumin seeds
1kg lean minced beef
3 tbsp tomato purée
1½ tsp light muscovado sugar
1 tsp dried oregano
300ml beef stock, hot
200g can chopped tomatoes
2 roasted red peppers from a jar, drained and chopped
400g can red kidney beans in water, rinsed and drained

For the spicy polenta cobbler
200g plain flour
1 tbsp baking powder
1 tbsp soft brown sugar
¼ tsp crushed dried chillies
75g polenta
65g Cheddar, finely grated
1 medium egg
175ml milk
2 tbsp sunflower oil
25g butter, melted

1. Heat the oil in a large pan, add the onions and garlic, and cook for 10 minutes, until lightly browned. Add the chillies and cumin, and fry for 2–3 minutes. Add the beef and cook over a high heat, breaking up with a wooden spoon as it browns. Add the purée, sugar, oregano, beef stock and tomatoes, and simmer for 25 minutes, until reduced and thickened. Stir in the peppers and kidney beans. Season, then spoon into a 2.75–3-litre shallow, oval ovenproof dish.

2. Preheat the oven to 220°C/fan 200°C/gas 7. Make the cobbler. Sift the flour, baking powder, sugar and ¼ teaspoon salt into a bowl, and stir in the chillies, polenta and 50g of the grated cheese. Beat the egg, milk, oil and melted butter together, and stir into the dry ingredients.

3. Drop 8 spoonfuls of the mixture around the edge of the dish, about 2.5cm apart, and sprinkle with the remaining grated cheese. Bake for 20 minutes, until bubbling hot and the topping is puffed up and golden.

Variations You could serve the mince and beans simply as chilli con carne with plain rice. Or wrap the mince in tortillas, sprinkle with Cheddar, bake until hot then top with soured cream or guacamole.

Keema pie

A simple and tasty dish that should appeal to traditional and more adventurous foodies alike.

SERVES 4
TAKES 30 MINUTES, PLUS
20 MINUTES IN THE OVEN

1 tbsp sunflower oil
1 red onion, finely chopped
2 garlic cloves, finely chopped
1 red chilli, seeded and finely chopped
Knob of fresh ginger, chopped
1 tsp cumin seeds
2 ripe tomatoes, roughly chopped
500g lean minced beef
2 tbsp madras curry paste
150ml chicken stock, hot
200g frozen peas
Juice of 1 lime
Mango chutney, to serve

For the mash
1kg sweet potatoes, cubed
4 tbsp soured cream
4 tbsp snipped fresh chives

1. Make the mash. Cook the sweet potatoes in a pan of boiling, lightly salted water for 15 minutes, until tender. Drain well, mash with the soured cream, seasoning and chives.

2. Meanwhile, heat the oil in a large frying pan over a medium heat. Add the onion, garlic, chilli and ginger, and cook, stirring occasionally, for 6–8 minutes, until golden. Add the cumin seeds, cook for 1 minute, then stir in the tomatoes, mince and curry paste, and cook for 5 minutes, until the tomatoes are pulpy. Add the stock and simmer for 10 minutes.

3. Preheat the oven to 200°C/fan 180°C/gas 6. Stir the peas and lime juice into the keema mix and season. Spoon into an ovenproof dish and top with the mash, roughing it up slightly. (You could freeze the dish at this point, if you wish.)

4. Transfer to a baking sheet and bake for 20 minutes, until the top is lightly browned. Serve with mango chutney. If you have frozen the dish, defrost thoroughly and bring it to room temperature before baking.

Variation Simply serve the curried mince with plain boiled rice or naan breads, if you prefer.

Quick beef and rosemary stew with dumplings

A traditional beef dish that can be enjoyed at any festive occasion or simply over the winter months.

SERVES 4
READY IN 30 MINUTES

2 tbsp olive oil
1 tbsp cornflour
1 tsp ground cinnamon
600g beef rump or sirloin, trimmed of excess fat and cut into large cubes
1 onion, sliced
1 carrot, thinly sliced
1 celery stick, thinly sliced
2 fresh rosemary sprigs, roughly torn
100ml red wine
500ml beef stock, hot
Grated zest and juice of 1 orange
Cooked peas, to serve

For the dumplings
150g self-raising flour
75g light vegetable suet
Handful of chopped fresh parsley

1. Heat half the oil in a casserole over a high heat. Mix the cornflour, cinnamon and some seasoning on a plate and dust the beef in the seasoned flour. Cook for 2–3 minutes, in batches, until browned all over. Transfer to a plate.

2. Heat the remaining oil in the casserole, add the onion, carrot, celery and rosemary, and stir-fry for 2–3 minutes. Add the wine, bubble until reduced by half, then add the stock and bring to the boil. Lower the heat until the stew is simmering, then add the orange zest and juice and the browned meat.

3. For the dumplings, mix the flour, suet, parsley, ½ teaspoon salt, and enough water in a large mixing bowl to make a soft dough. Roughly shape into 8 balls, dropping them into the stew as you go. Simmer gently for 10 minutes, until they've puffed up. Serve hot, with some cooked peas.

S

Stuffed beef rolls with tomato and olive sauce

Roll some beef steaks around a gorgeous stuffing and fry in a rich tomato sauce to make this easy recipe for the family.

SERVES 4
READY IN 45 MINUTES

50g butter
2 small onions, 1 finely chopped and 1 finely sliced
½ tsp dried mixed herbs
75g fresh white breadcrumbs
4 x 160–180g thin-cut beef frying steaks
1 tbsp olive oil
1 garlic clove, crushed
400g can chopped tomatoes in natural juice
10 pitted black olives, sliced
Small handful of chopped fresh parsley
Mashed or boiled potatoes, to serve

1. Melt the butter in a large frying pan over a medium–low heat. Add the chopped onion and cook gently for 5 minutes, until softened. Add the herbs and cook for another minute. Stir in the breadcrumbs and season. Tip the stuffing mix into a bowl.

2. Lay 1 steak on a board and spread with a quarter of the stuffing. Roll up to encase the stuffing and secure in place with a cocktail stick. Repeat with the remaining beef and stuffing.

3. Add the oil to the frying pan and return to a high heat. Brown each stuffed beef roll all over for a few minutes, then remove and set aside.

4. Add the sliced onion and garlic to the pan, and cook over a medium heat for 5 minutes, until softened and starting to colour. Return the beef to the pan and pour over the chopped tomatoes. Half-fill the empty can with water and add this as well. Scatter with the olives, bring to the boil and simmer for 20 minutes, stirring occasionally, until cooked through and the sauce has reduced slightly. Garnish with the parsley, season to taste and serve with mashed or boiled potatoes.

★ DELICIOUS. TIP Freeze any leftovers, then thaw completely before reheating in the oven or microwave until piping hot.

Red beef stew

This wonderfully meaty beef stew recipe is ideal for making in advance and having on standby in the freezer.

SERVES 8

TAKES 1½ HOURS, PLUS COOLING

4 tbsp vegetable oil
900g lean stewing beef steak, diced
2 onions, chopped
2 tbsp paprika
1 garlic clove, crushed
1 jar tomato sauce for pasta
1 tsp concentrated beef stock or ½ beef stock cube
2 red peppers, seeded and cut into chunks
250g button mushrooms, halved
1 large sweet potato, cut into big chunks
Soured cream and jacket potatoes, to serve

1. Heat the oil in a large casserole over a medium-high heat. Fry the beef in batches until just browned. Remove with a slotted spoon and set aside in a bowl.

2. Add the onions to the casserole and cook for 5 minutes, stirring, until just transparent. Stir in the paprika and garlic, cook for 1 minute, then pour in the tomato sauce. Fill the jar with hot water and add to the casserole. Stir in the stock concentrate or cube, then add the peppers, mushrooms and sweet potato. Return the beef to the casserole and bring to the boil. Simmer over a medium-low heat for 1 hour, or until the meat is tender.

3. Cool completely, then freeze in portions for up to 3 months. Thaw for 24 hours in the fridge. To reheat, put the stew into a large pan over a medium heat and heat until piping hot or defrost and reheat in the microwave, according to portion size.

4. Season to taste and serve with soured cream and jacket potatoes.

★ DELICIOUS. TIP If you want to eat this straight away, prepare up to the end of step 2, then skip step 3 and complete step 4.

Stir-fried beef with noodles and oyster sauce

An Asian-inspired stir-fry recipe to savour, which includes tasty marinated beef and filling noodles.

SERVES 2
READY IN 25 MINUTES

225g lean beef steak (sirloin or rump), cut into strips
2 tsp light soy sauce
2 tsp sesame oil, plus a few tbsp for the noodles
2 tsp dry sherry
1 tsp cornflour
1 red pepper
Small bunch of spring onions
150g medium or thin dried egg noodles
3 tbsp oyster sauce

1. Put the beef in a bowl with the soy sauce, sesame oil, sherry and cornflour, mix well and set aside for 10 minutes.

2. Meanwhile, seed the pepper, cut into thin strips and set aside. Finely shred the spring onions and set aside.

3. Soak the noodles in a bowl of boiling water for a few minutes, until tender. Drain, refresh and toss with the extra sesame oil.

4. Heat a wok until very hot and stir-fry the beef for 5 minutes until seared all over. Tip into a sieve to drain away the oil and set aside. Put the wok back on to the heat, add the pepper and stir-fry for 1–2 minutes. Remove and set aside. Add the oyster sauce to the wok and bring to a simmer, then add the beef and noodles, and toss together. Add the pepper and onions, toss through and serve.

Layered cottage pie

This dish is inexpensive to make for four people and the sliced potatoes make a sophisticated change from the usual mashed variety.

SERVES 4
TAKES 30 MINUTES, PLUS
30 MINUTES IN THE OVEN

1 tbsp olive oil
1 large onion, finely sliced
500g beef mince
3 tbsp tomato purée
2 tbsp tomato ketchup
1 tbsp Worcestershire sauce
1.2kg potatoes, cut into 5mm slices
25g Cheddar, grated

1. Heat the oil in a pan and gently fry the onion for 5 minutes. Add the mince and fry until browned all over.

2. Stir in the tomato purée, ketchup and Worcestershire sauce. Add a splash of hot water and season. Simmer gently for 15–20 minutes.

3. Meanwhile, preheat the oven to 200°C/fan 180°C/gas 6. Put the potatoes in a pan of water. Bring to the boil, then simmer for 2–3 minutes. Drain, then layer half in a baking dish. Spoon the mince over the potatoes, then layer over the remaining potatoes. Sprinkle with cheese and bake for 30 minutes, then serve.

Variation For chilli con carne, add 1 teaspoon each of chilli powder, ground cumin and coriander, and a can of kidney beans to the mince. Serve with rice and soured cream.

Spiced meatball curry

You can freeze this delicious curry for up to 3 months, or just freeze the raw meatballs, then defrost them thoroughly and finish the recipe.

SERVES 4
READY IN ABOUT 1 HOUR

450g beef mince
1 small onion, roughly grated
2.5cm piece fresh ginger, grated
2 garlic cloves, finely chopped
1 tbsp ground coriander
½ tsp ground cumin
1–1½ tsp cayenne pepper
Bunch of fresh coriander, chopped (reserve a few leaves to garnish)
Naan breads, to serve

For the sauce

1 tbsp sunflower oil
2 onions, finely chopped
2 tbsp tikka masala curry paste
6 large tomatoes, chopped
300ml vegetable stock, hot

1. Put the beef, onion, ginger, garlic, spices and fresh coriander in a large bowl and mix together well. With clean wet hands, form the mixture into about 30 balls and chill for 30 minutes while you prepare the sauce.

2. To make the sauce, heat the oil in a large frying pan and fry the onions for 8 minutes, until soft and golden. Add the curry paste and fry for a minute, then stir in the tomatoes and stock. Simmer for 15 minutes, until the sauce begins to thicken.

3. Sit the meatballs in the sauce and simmer for 25–30 minutes, turning occasionally, until cooked. Scatter with extra coriander and serve with naans.

★ DELICIOUS. TIP Freeze the cooled, finished curry in a plastic container for up to 3 months. Defrost before reheating until piping hot.

chicken

Chicken puttanesca with polenta

This delicious one-dish Italian dinner uses ready-prepared ingredients and so requires almost no effort to put together.

SERVES 2
TAKES 5 MINUTES, PLUS
25 MINUTES IN THE OVEN

350g ready-made polenta
10g ready-grated Parmesan
350g jar tomato sauce
Handful of cherry tomatoes
Handful of pitted black olives
1 tbsp capers, drained and rinsed
2 free-range chicken breasts, skin on
Fresh basil leaves, to serve

1. Preheat the oven to 220°C/fan 200°C/gas 7. In a large ovenproof dish, break up the ready-made polenta into chunks, sprinkle with Parmesan and season. Spoon over the tomato sauce and scatter with cherry tomatoes, black olives and capers.

2. Top with the chicken breasts. Season, drizzle with a little olive oil and bake in the oven for 25 minutes, or until the chicken is cooked through. Serve sprinkled with fresh basil leaves.

Variation Not keen on polenta? Substitute it with diced butternut squash and roast in the same way.

Coq au vin

A tasty one-pot recipe for the classic chicken dish – eat some and freeze the rest.

SERVES 4
TAKES ABOUT 30 MINUTES, 30 MINUTES IN THE OVEN, PLUS OVERNIGHT MARINATING AND COOLING

75cl bottle good red wine
4 tbsp brandy
12 pickling onions or small shallots, unpeeled
4 free-range chicken thighs and 4 drumsticks, skin on
2 celery sticks, thickly sliced
2 medium carrots, thickly sliced
2 garlic cloves, bruised
2 bay leaves
A?few fresh thyme sprigs, plus extra to garnish
25g plain flour, seasoned, plus 1 tbsp
1 tbsp olive oil
15g butter
2 x 70g packs diced pancetta (or use chopped streaky bacon)
250g chestnut mushrooms, wiped clean and halved if large
Small handful of chopped fresh parsley, to garnish
Mashed potato, to serve

1. Pour the wine and brandy into a pan and boil for 5 minutes, until reduced by a third. Set aside. Place the onions in a bowl, pour over boiling water and leave for 5 minutes. Drain, cool, peel and halve. Put in a bowl with the chicken, celery, carrots, garlic, bay and thyme. Pour over the wine, turn to coat. Cover and chill overnight, turning occasionally.

2. The next day, preheat the oven to 180°C/fan 160°C/gas 4. Drain the chicken, reserving the wine. Pat dry the chicken on kitchen paper. Toss in the seasoned flour to coat.

3. Heat the oil and butter in a large casserole over a medium heat. Add the pancetta and cook, stirring occasionally, for 3–4 minutes, until golden. Remove with a slotted spoon and set aside.

4. Add the chicken to the hot casserole (in a snug, single layer), and cook for 5 minutes, turning occasionally, until browned all over. Remove and set aside.

5. Add the drained vegetables and herbs to the casserole with the mushrooms and cook, stirring, for 3–4 minutes. Add 1 tablespoon flour, cook for 1 minute, then slowly stir in the wine. Season, return the chicken and pancetta to the pan, and bring to the boil. Cover and cook in the oven for 30 minutes. Garnish with parsley and serve with mash.

★ DELICIOUS. TIP To freeze: transfer to a container and freeze for up to 3 months. Defrost at room temperature for 10 hours, or in the fridge for 24 hours. Bring to room temperature. Reheat over a medium heat for 10 minutes, until piping hot.

Biryani-style baked chicken and rice

A twist on a classic Indian dish that's packed with fresh flavours and vibrant veg.

SERVES 4
TAKES 20 MINUTES, PLUS ABOUT 30 MINUTES IN THE OVEN

2 tbsp olive oil
8 chicken thighs, bone in and skin on
1 large onion, finely chopped
3 garlic cloves, sliced
2 tsp garam masala
1 tsp ground ginger
1 green chilli, finely sliced
300g basmati rice
650ml chicken stock, hot
200g frozen mixed green vegetables
2 tbsp chopped fresh flatleaf parsley

1. Preheat the oven to 190°C/fan 170°C/ gas 5. Heat the oil in a large roasting tin on the hob. Add the chicken and fry over a high heat until golden brown all over. Remove and set aside.

2. Add the onion and cook gently for 6–8 minutes. Stir in the garlic, garam masala, ginger and chilli. Stir in the rice and cook for 1 minute. Top with the chicken and pour over the stock.

3. Cover with foil and bake for 20 minutes, until the rice has nearly absorbed all of the stock. Add a dash of hot water if the rice looks dry. Uncover and stir in the frozen vegetables. Re-cover and bake for 8–10 minutes, until everything is cooked. Scatter with parsley to serve.

Variation Use tender lamb fillet instead of chicken: cut into small cubes and fry as in step 1. You could also use cold cooked lamb left over from Sunday lunch.

Chicken and preserved lemon tagine

This is one of the best-known and most-loved tagines. Accompany with houmous, flatbread and a few mezze dishes to make it into a dinner-party spread.

SERVES 4–6
READY IN 1 HOUR 20 MINUTES

Pinch of saffron strands
600ml chicken stock, hot
2 tbsp olive oil
1.7kg organic chicken, jointed, or 1.5kg chicken pieces (leg, thigh and breast)
1 large onion, chopped
3 garlic cloves, finely chopped
1 tsp ground ginger
½ tsp coriander seeds, lightly crushed
1 cinnamon stick, snapped in half
5 small preserved lemons, quartered
200g green olives
Small handful of fresh flatleaf parsley or coriander, chopped
Couscous, to serve

1. Soak the saffron in a jug with the hot stock for a few minutes.

2. Meanwhile, heat the olive oil in a large deep-sided frying pan or casserole over a high heat and brown the chicken pieces for 2–3 minutes. You may need to do this in batches. Remove the chicken to a plate and add the onion to the pan. Reduce the heat and cook, stirring occasionally, for 5 minutes.

3. Add the garlic and spices to the pan, and cook, stirring, for a further minute. If you're using a tagine, transfer the onion to the base and add the saffron-infused stock and the browned chicken pieces (if using a casserole, leave the onion in the pan, then add the chicken and stock). Bring to the boil and simmer over a gentle heat, covered, for 40–50 minutes, until the chicken is tender.

4. Add the lemons and olives, and simmer for a further 15 minutes. Season to taste, scatter with the fresh herbs and serve with couscous.

★ DELICIOUS. TIP You can easily cook the tagine in a large casserole in the oven, if you prefer. Preheat the oven to 150°C/fan 130°C/gas 2 and cook, covered, for 1 hour. Add the lemon and olives, and return to the oven for a further 15 minutes before scattering with parsley and coriander.

All-in-one baked lemon and rosemary chicken

This super-simple one-pot chicken recipe requires almost no preparation and is ready in less than an hour.

SERVES 4
TAKES 10 MINUTES, PLUS 40–50 MINUTES IN THE OVEN

8 chicken portions (use legs, thighs and breasts)
500g new potatoes, halved lengthways
2 lemons, cut into wedges
4 fresh rosemary sprigs
A glass of white wine
4 tbsp olive oil
Seasonal vegetables, to serve

1. Put the chicken portions into a roasting tin with the new potatoes, lemons, fresh rosemary sprigs, white wine and olive oil, and season well.

2. Bake, uncovered, in a preheated oven at 180°C/fan 160°C/gas 4 for 40–50 minutes, until tender and golden. Serve with seasonal vegetables.

Pot au feu

The chicken and vegetables slowly simmer in a pot for an hour and a half to extract maximum flavour. This recipe is comforting in many ways, being low in calories, fat and salt.

SERVES 6
READY IN 2 HOURS

1kg whole free-range chicken
6 large Chantenay carrots, trimmed
2 medium onions, each cut into 6 wedges
2 celery sticks, each cut into 4 lengths
100g pearl barley
20g fresh flatleaf parsley, stalks and leaves separated and chopped
20 black peppercorns
4 fresh bay leaves
4–5 fresh thyme sprigs
1 litre good-quality vegetable stock, hot
¼ white cabbage, shredded
Crusty bread or boiled potatoes, to serve

1. Place the chicken in a large, snug-fitting saucepan. Add the carrots, onions, celery, pearl barley, parsley stalks, peppercorns, bay leaves and thyme. Pour over the stock, along with 1 litre cold water.

2. Slowly bring to the boil, cover and simmer gently for 1 hour, then uncover and simmer gently for 30 minutes.

3. Place a wooden spoon in the chicken's cavity and carefully lift it out. Remove as many peppercorns, bay leaves, thyme and parsley stalks as you can from the stock.

4. Using a ladle, skim off any scum or fat from the surface. Use a fork to remove the flesh of the chicken from the carcass. Discard the skin and add the meat to the stock, with the parsley leaves and shredded cabbage.

5. Bring the stock back to the boil, taste, then adjust the seasoning if necessary. Serve with crusty bread or boiled potatoes.

Spanish chicken and rice

Give this speedy and tasty paella a go. You could use chicken thighs for this recipe, as they're often cheaper than breasts.

SERVES 4
READY IN 25 MINUTES

- 2 tbsp olive oil
- 4 chicken breasts, skin on
- 1 onion, roughly chopped
- 2 garlic cloves, crushed
- 100g chorizo, cut into chunks
- 2 tsp smoked paprika
- 2 x 250g packs ready-cooked basmati rice
- 250g roasted peppers, drained and thickly sliced
- Handful of pitted Spanish olives
- Handful of fresh flatleaf parsley leaves, roughly chopped

1. Heat the olive oil in a large sauté pan over a medium heat. Season the chicken breasts and add to the pan, skin-side down. Brown for 10 minutes, turning halfway through, then push to the edge of the pan.

2. Add the onion, garlic, chorizo and smoked paprika. Cook for 5 minutes, until the onion has softened.

3. Add the basmati rice and roasted peppers, mix everything together, and cook for 3 minutes, stirring, to heat through. Add a handful of pitted Spanish olives and scatter with a handful of fresh flatleaf parsley leaves, roughly chopped, to serve.

Lemon roast chicken with peppers

A cheap and incredibly easy to prepare midweek meal that's ideal for casual entertaining with family or friends.

SERVES 4
TAKES 15 MINUTES, PLUS 30–35 MINUTES IN THE OVEN

1.8–2kg free-range chicken, jointed into 8 pieces
2 tbsp olive oil
1 garlic bulb, cloves separated but not peeled
1 red and 1 yellow pepper, seeded and sliced
Zest and juice of 1 lemon
2 fresh rosemary sprigs
Splash of white wine
100ml chicken stock
Mash and steamed greens, to serve

1. Preheat the oven to 200°C/fan 180°C/gas 6. Put the chicken pieces into a large roasting tin with the olive oil, garlic, red and yellow peppers, lemon zest and juice and rosemary sprigs.

2. Add the wine and chicken stock, season and roast for 30–35 minutes, until cooked. Serve with mash and steamed greens.

★ DELICIOUS. TIP Using a whole chicken and jointing it into 8 pieces is much more cost-effective than buying the pieces separately, and you get a lot more flavour than from chicken breasts alone.

Pot-roast guinea fowl with pistachio stuffing

Guinea fowl is not just a pot roast; this succulent bird makes a classy centrepiece to a dinner table.

SERVES 2 GENEROUSLY
READY IN 2 HOURS

- 1 (about 1kg) guinea fowl with giblets
- 2 rashers dry-cured smoked streaky bacon
- 200g coarsely minced pork
- Leaves of 1 fresh rosemary sprig
- 2 garlic cloves
- 50g shelled pistachios
- 2 tbsp brandy
- 2 outer leaves of a Savoy cabbage or cavolo nero
- 1 tbsp butter, softened
- 2 tbsp olive oil
- 6 small shallots, peeled and left whole
- 1 celery stick, roughly sliced
- 2 carrots, thickly sliced
- 1 tbsp plain flour
- 100ml white wine
- 1 tbsp tomato purée

1. Remove the giblets from the guinea fowl, then chop the liver very finely with the bacon. Discard the rest of the giblets. Add the liver and bacon to a large bowl with the pork mince. Chop the rosemary and garlic with the pistachios, and fold into the meat. Season with salt and pepper and stir in the brandy. Chill until needed.

2. Soak the cabbage leaves in a bowl of boiling water for 2 minutes, drain, then plunge into a bowl of cold water. Drain again and pat dry with kitchen paper. Divide the stuffing mixture between the cabbage leaves, wrapping the leaves around the meat and shaping to make 2 neat round packages.

3. Lightly season the bird's cavity and pop in the leaf-wrapped stuffing. Smear the butter over the outside of the bird and season with more salt.

4. Heat the olive oil in a casserole or large pot with a lid over a medium–high heat, and brown the guinea fowl all over. Transfer the bird to a plate, then add the shallots, sliced celery and carrots to the casserole or pot and fry quite briskly for 10 minutes, allowing them to caramelise slightly.

5. Add the flour, cook for 1 minute, then add the wine, tomato purée and 200ml water. Return the bird to the pot, breast-side up. Cover, reduce the heat to medium–low and simmer for about 1¼ hours. To test the bird is cooked, pierce the leg to check the juices run clear. Allow the cooked bird to rest in the gravy for 10 minutes before carving.

Roasted pesto chicken with polenta and vegetables

This is a very economical and quick dish to prepare on a weeknight. All the family will love the rich, comforting flavours, and you'll probably have most of the ingredients in the fridge!

SERVES 4
TAKES 15 MINUTES, PLUS 45 MINUTES IN THE OVEN

2 tbsp olive oil
8 chicken thighs
2 tbsp green pesto
500g packet ready-made polenta, cut into cubes
1 large courgette, roughly chopped
150g tomatoes, roughly chopped

1. Preheat the oven to 200°C/fan 180°C/gas 6. Heat the olive oil in a roasting tin over a high heat. Add the chicken, in batches, and brown on all sides. Set the chicken aside on a plate. Tip the cooking juices into a bowl and mix with 1 tablespoon of the pesto.

2. Arrange the polenta and courgette in the roasting tin. Make spaces in between and add the browned chicken thighs. Drizzle with the pesto pan juices and roast in the oven for 35 minutes.

3. Remove from the oven and scatter with the tomatoes. Return to the oven and roast for a further 10 minutes. Drizzle the chicken and vegetables with the remaining pesto and divide among plates to serve.

fish and seafood

One-pan roast fish

Fresh and healthy but with real flavour, this is a great dish to light up the winter months.

SERVES 4
TAKES 15 MINUTES, PLUS
35–40 MINUTES IN THE OVEN

Olive oil for drizzling, plus
 1 tbsp
2 red onions, cut into wedges
2 garlic cloves, sliced
450g waxy potatoes
Knob of butter
4 tomatoes, sliced
1 tbsp chopped fresh
 flatleaf parsley
Leaves of 2 fresh tarragon sprigs
4 skinless white fish fillets,
 such as haddock or pollack
Juice of 1 lemon, plus 4 slices

1. Preheat the oven to 180°C/fan 160°C/gas 4. Heat 1 tablespoon olive oil in a roasting tin over a low heat and fry the onions for 5 minutes. Add the garlic and cook for a further 2 minutes. Tip into a bowl and set aside.

2. Peel and slice the potatoes and layer in the roasting tin. Drizzle with olive oil, dot with butter and season. Roast for 25 minutes.

3. Pile the cooked onions and garlic on to the potatoes, then top with the tomatoes, parsley, tarragon leaves and fish fillets.

4. Drizzle with olive oil and the juice of 1 lemon. Season well, top with lemon slices and bake for 12–15 minutes, until the fish is cooked through.

Roast cod with bacon, tomatoes and basil

For a tasty, guilt-free supper, use sustainably caught cod to make this dish.

SERVES 4
TAKES 10 MINUTES, PLUS 12–15 MINUTES IN THE OVEN

Olive oil, for drizzling
4 sustainably caught cod steaks, with skin
2–4 rashers streaky bacon
250g mini plum tomatoes, halved
Balsamic vinegar, for splashing over
Handful of fresh basil leaves, to garnish

1. Drizzle a little oil over the base of a roasting tin and add the cod steaks, skin-side down. Cut the rashers of streaky bacon into small pieces and scatter over the fish with the mini plum tomatoes. Season and add a splash of balsamic vinegar over each cod steak.

2. Bake in a preheated oven at 200°C/fan 180°C/gas 6 for 12–15 minutes, until the fish is just cooked. Scatter with a handful of fresh basil leaves to serve.

Deluxe fish pie

It's worth seeking out an Arbroath smokie for this pie. If you're using potted shrimps, you won't need the nutmeg as they contain mace.

SERVES 4
READY IN 1½ HOURS

- 1 Arbroath smokie or 150g undyed smoked haddock fillet
- 100g small cooked and peeled prawns or potted shrimps
- 1 medium whole cooked crab or 2 dressed crabs or 115g tub each of brown and white crab meat
- 4 big or 8 small scallops (optional)
- 700g floury potatoes, roughly diced
- 1 tbsp mild oil (such as rapeseed)
- 1 leek, washed and roughly chopped
- 2 celery sticks, roughly chopped
- 2 tbsp unsalted butter
- 1 heaped tbsp plain flour
- 200ml milk, plus extra for mashing (optional)
- 100ml double cream
- Pinch of freshly grated nutmeg
- Tiny pinch of saffron strands
- 3 hard-boiled eggs

1. Split and flake the smokie, discarding the bones. If using smoked haddock, skin, bone and dice, then set aside. If using potted shrimps, melt the butter and strain out the shrimps. Set aside. If using a whole crab, crack the shell and claws, pick out the white and brown meat, and separate. Cut large scallops, if using, into 2 or 3 discs.

2. Boil the potatoes in plenty of salted water for 15–20 minutes, until cooked. Drain and set aside.

3. Heat the oil and gently fry the leek and celery for 8–10 minutes until tender, without browning. Add the smokie (or haddock), prawns or shrimps, the scallops and white crab meat. Stir for 1–2 minutes, remove from the heat, cover and rest in the pan.

4. Meanwhile, heat 1 tablespoon of the butter in a pan. Add the flour, stir and cook for a minute, then remove from the heat and gradually whisk in the milk and cream. Cook until thickened, then stir in the nutmeg and saffron. Combine with the fish.

5. Preheat the oven to 200°C/fan 180°C/gas 6. Peel and chop the eggs, then add to the pie filling. Mix the potatoes with the remaining butter, a little milk, if you like, and the brown crab meat. Mash thoroughly and season.

6. Fill a 1.2-litre dish with the fish mix, then spread the potato topping over. Bake for 20–25 minutes, until the filling is bubbling and the top is golden.

Variation For a plainer version, use all white fish, or a mixture of white fish, salmon and smoked haddock.

Coriander and beer mussels

The Thai twist makes this an amazing bowl of mussels. Quick enough for midweek, but special enough for entertaining too.

SERVES 4
READY IN 25 MINUTES

3kg fresh live mussels
2 medium onions, finely chopped
1 tbsp sunflower oil
1 medium red chilli, seeded and finely chopped
2 garlic cloves, finely chopped
1 lemongrass stalk, finely chopped
4cm piece fresh ginger, grated
500ml lager
30g fresh coriander, chopped
Juice of 1 lime, plus lime wedges to serve
Crusty bread, to serve

1. Rinse the mussels in cold water, removing the beards. Throw away any that have broken shells or that don't close when tapped.

2. Place the onions in a large, deep pan with 250ml boiling water and bubble over a high heat for 5 minutes, until the water is reduced.

3. Add the oil, chilli, garlic, lemongrass and ginger, and stir until the onions turn slightly golden. Add the lager and simmer for 2 minutes. Add the mussels and cover tightly with a lid. Simmer for 3–5 minutes or until all the mussels have opened, shaking the pan occasionally.

4. Discard any mussels that haven't opened. Add the coriander and lime juice, and serve with lime wedges to squeeze over and some crusty bread.

Variation To make traditional moules, omit the lager, chillies, lemongrass, ginger and coriander and use white wine and parsley instead.

Piquant monkfish

Low in calories, fat and carbs, this recipe tastes fabulous and will keep you looking that way.

SERVES 4
TAKES 15 MINUTES, PLUS
20 MINUTES IN THE OVEN

4 anchovy fillets, finely chopped
2 tbsp capers, rinsed and chopped
20g fresh flatleaf parsley, leaves picked and roughly chopped
Grated zest of 2 lemons
8 slices Parma ham
4 x 125g–150g monkfish fillets
300g cherry tomatoes on the vine
2 red onions, each cut into 8 wedges
1 tbsp olive oil
1 tbsp aged balsamic vinegar
100g wild rocket leaves, to serve

1. Preheat the oven to 200°C/fan 180°C/gas 6. In a bowl, mix together the anchovies, capers, parsley and lemon zest. Season.

2. Slightly overlap 2 slices of Parma ham lengthways. Spread a quarter of the anchovy mixture down the middle. Top with a fish fillet and wrap the ham around to enclose it. Repeat with the remaining ham and fish.

3. Place the tomatoes and onions on a large baking sheet, drizzle with the oil and bake for 5 minutes. Add the fish parcels to the tray and roast for 15 minutes, until cooked through.

4. Remove the monkfish parcels to a warm plate and pour the vinegar over the tomatoes and onions. Divide the tomatoes, onions and monkfish among plates. Drizzle with any juices from the baking sheet and scatter with rocket to serve.

Halibut, ratatouille and new potato tray bake

The combination of baked halibut, new potatoes and ratatouille makes this a wonderful summer dish.

SERVES 4
TAKES 15 MINUTES, PLUS 45 MINUTES IN THE OVEN

- 4 tbsp olive oil, plus extra for drizzling
- 1 garlic clove, roughly chopped
- 500g fresh tomatoes, roughly chopped
- 1 red onion, cut into about 3cm cubes
- 1 red pepper, seeded and cut into about 3cm cubes
- 1 aubergine, cut into about 3cm cubes
- 1–2 courgettes, cut into about 3cm cubes
- 2 tbsp oregano, leaves roughly chopped
- 4 tbsp chopped parsley
- 500g waxy small new potatoes
- 2 tbsp baby capers, rinsed and drained
- 1 red chilli, chopped or a good pinch of chilli flakes
- 4 (about 200g each) halibut steaks
- 1 lemon, finely sliced

1. Preheat the oven to 200°C/fan 180°C/gas 6. In a roasting tin, place 2 tablespoons oil, the garlic, tomatoes, vegetables and herbs in a single layer and toss together. Roast the ratatouille for 30 minutes until tender.

2. Meanwhile, thinly slice the potatoes and place in a large bowl. Toss with the remaining 2 tablespoons olive oil, plenty of black pepper and a small pinch of salt. Arrange in a single layer on a large baking sheet or in a dish and bake for 20 minutes or until golden.

3. Spoon the ratatouille on top of the potatoes and sprinkle with the capers and chilli.

4. Place the halibut on top of the ratatouille and layer the lemon slices over the fish. Drizzle with a little more oil. Season well and bake for 15 minutes, until the fish is cooked through.

Salmon with simple white wine and thyme risotto

A warming dish made from pan-fried salmon paired with a light herby risotto.

SERVES 4
TAKES 25 MINUTES, PLUS 10–12 MINUTES IN THE OVEN

2 tbsp olive oil
600g piece skinless boneless salmon fillet
Small knob of butter
1 large onion, chopped
2 garlic cloves, chopped
4 fresh thyme sprigs
400g carnaroli or arborio risotto rice
250ml dry white wine, ideally Italian
1 litre good chicken stock, hot

1. Heat 1 tablespoon oil in a large frying pan over a medium heat and pan-fry the salmon for 3–4 minutes on each side. Set aside to rest.

2. Wipe out the pan and heat the remaining olive oil and butter over a medium heat. Add the onion, garlic and thyme, and cook, stirring occasionally, for 5 minutes, until the onion has softened.

3. Stir in the rice and cook for 1 minute. Add the wine and cook vigorously for 2–3 minutes, until evaporated. Pour in the stock, a third at a time, adding more when the last is absorbed, and simmer gently for 15 minutes, stirring regularly, until all the liquid has evaporated and the rice is creamy and just tender.

4. Flake the cooked salmon over the top of the risotto and leave to heat through. Grind over plenty of black pepper and serve.

Variation Try this risotto with prawns: make the risotto and add uncooked prawns for the last 5 minutes of cooking time until they have turned pink. Use parsley instead of thyme.

Mussels, squid and prawn stew with harissa

Even without the harissa, this seafood dish of mussels, squid and prawns would be a blissful fish stew for a blustery day. Adding it only enhances the flavour.

SERVES 4
READY IN ABOUT 1 HOUR

300g whole raw cold-water prawns, shells on
1kg fresh live mussels
200g fresh squid, cleaned
3 tbsp mild olive oil
1 shallot, finely chopped
3 celery sticks, finely diced
1 carrot, finely diced
1 leek, trimmed, washed and finely diced
250ml dry white wine
1–2 tbsp harissa (depending on taste), plus extra to serve
1 tsp tomato purée
Small pinch of saffron strands
Small bunch of fresh coriander or flatleaf parsley, to serve

1. Peel the prawns, then pop the shells and heads in a pot with 500ml water. Bring to a simmer (don't boil) and let it fizz gently for about 45 minutes. Chill the peeled prawns.

2. Meanwhile, scrape the barnacles and pull any beards from the mussels. Run them under a cold tap for a minute or so, then discard any open mussels that don't close when tapped on the worktop, along with any that are cracked. Chill.

3. Slice the squid bodies into rings and chop the tentacles, if you wish. Chill.

4. Heat the oil in a large pot (preferably one with a lid) over a medium–low heat. Add the vegetables and cook for 5 minutes, stirring occasionally, until they begin to soften. Stir in the wine, harissa, tomato purée and saffron, and simmer gently for 15–20 minutes, until reduced by about two-thirds.

5. Once the liquid has reduced, add the prawns, mussels and squid. Strain the prawn-shell stock and add about 300ml to the pot. Cover and allow everything to steam for about 5 minutes or until the fish is cooked and all the mussels are open. Discard any that don't open after cooking.

6. Check the seasoning. Divide among bowls (don't leave any of that stock and mussel liquor behind – it's fantastic) and garnish with coriander or parsley sprigs. Serve with a bowl of more harissa to stir in, if you like a little extra spice.

Russian fish pie

Prepare this attractive fish pie and eat immediately or freeze it for later. It's perfect for entertaining.

SERVES 6–8
TAKES 20 MINUTES, 25 MINUTES TO COOK, PLUS FREEZING AND 1¼ HOURS BAKING FROM FROZEN

- Knob of butter
- 1 tbsp olive oil
- 1 large onion, finely chopped
- 150g chestnut mushrooms, chopped
- 1 tsp ground turmeric
- 100g freshly cooked basmati rice
- Bunch of fresh dill, chopped
- Bunch of fresh parsley, chopped
- 1 tbsp capers, drained, rinsed and chopped
- Zest of 1 lemon
- 2 large free-range eggs, hard-boiled and chopped, plus 1 beaten free-range egg, for glazing
- Plain flour, for dusting
- 2 x 500g packs fresh puff pastry
- 800g piece salmon tail fillet

1. Heat the butter and oil in a pan over a low heat and cook the onion for 5–6 minutes. Add the mushrooms and cook for 5–8 minutes. Stir in the turmeric and cook for 1 minute, then add the rice, herbs, capers, lemon zest and chopped egg. Season and cool.

2. Preheat the oven to 200°C/fan 180°C/gas 6. On a floured board, roll out 1 piece of pastry to pound-coin thickness and trim to a 30cm x 20cm rectangle. Put on a large baking sheet and place the salmon on the pastry. Season, then arrange the rice mixture on top. Brush the pastry edges with beaten egg.

3. Roll out the remaining pastry, so it will generously cover the salmon, and lay over the top. Trim, leaving a 2cm border, and press the pastry together to seal. Use any pastry trimmings to decorate the top, then bake for 35–40 minutes.

★ DELICIOUS. TIP To freeze: wrap cling film around the cooled pie and baking sheet, and freeze for up to 3 months. To serve, preheat the oven to 180°C/fan 160°C/gas 4. Bake from frozen for 1 hour 5 minutes, then turn up the oven to 220°C/fan 200°C/gas 7 and cook for a further 10 minutes, until cooked.

vegetarian

Creamy mushroom and chestnut filo pie

This rustic vegetarian pie is delicious eaten on the day or can be frozen, then defrosted and cooked from room temperature.

SERVES 4
TAKES 30 MINUTES, PLUS COOLING

100g butter, melted
2 leeks, trimmed, washed and sliced
2 garlic cloves, crushed
750g mixed mushrooms (we used girolle, chestnut and oyster), wiped clean and thickly sliced
150ml dry white wine
200g pack cooked chestnuts, roughly chopped
142ml carton double cream
Juice of ½ small lemon
Leaves from a few fresh thyme sprigs
8 fresh filo pastry sheets
Steamed spring greens, to serve

1. Melt 40g of the butter in a large, deep frying pan over a medium heat. Add the leeks and garlic, and cook for 3–4 minutes, stirring occasionally, until they begin to soften. Add the mushrooms, increase the heat to high and stir-fry for 2–3 minutes, until wilted slightly.

2. Add the wine to the pan and bubble until nearly all of it has evaporated. Reduce the heat to medium–low and stir in the chestnuts, cream, lemon juice and half the thyme leaves. Simmer gently for a few minutes, until the sauce has reduced a little, then season to taste. Transfer to a deep 1.5-litre ovenproof dish and cool completely.

3. Preheat the oven to 190°C/fan 170°C/gas 5. Stir the rest of the thyme into the remaining melted butter. Brush half the filo pastry sheets with some of the thyme butter, lay 1 unbuttered filo sheet on top of 1 buttered filo sheet, then brush again with thyme butter. Halve each filo pile through the middle, so you have 8 smaller squares. Overlap the squares over the filling.

4. At this point, freeze or continue cooking to eat immediately. Cook for 25 minutes or until the filling is piping hot and the pastry is golden. Serve with steamed spring greens.

Variation If you want to make a meaty version, add chopped bacon to the mixture.

Summer vegetable tagine

Vary the vegetables you use for this more-ish Moorish vegetarian dish, according to what's in season.

SERVES 4–6
READY IN 40 MINUTES

- 2 tbsp olive oil
- 12 shallots, peeled and halved if large (see tip)
- 2 garlic cloves, finely chopped
- 4cm piece fresh ginger, finely chopped
- 150g brown or green lentils
- 2 tsp ras el-hanout
- ½ tsp cumin seeds
- 800ml vegetable stock, hot
- 100g dried ready-to-eat apricots
- 150g baby carrots, scrubbed
- 3 small fennel bulbs, each cut into 6 wedges, any herby fronds chopped and set aside
- 2 courgettes, halved lengthways and cut into 4cm wedges
- 200g fresh or frozen peas
- Grated zest of 2 lemons, plus the juice of 1
- 100g blanched almonds, toasted and chopped
- Handful of fresh flatleaf parsley, chopped

1. Heat the oil in a large tagine base, casserole or saucepan. Add the shallots and cook, stirring, for 3 minutes. Add the garlic, ginger, lentils, ras el-hanout and cumin, and cook for a further minute. Pour in the stock and bring to the boil, then reduce the heat slightly, cover and simmer for 15 minutes.

2. Add the apricots, carrots, fennel wedges and courgettes, and simmer, covered, for 5 minutes. Add the peas and half the lemon zest, and cook for 5 more minutes. Stir in the lemon juice and season to taste.

3. Scatter with the remaining zest, toasted almonds, fennel tops and parsley to serve.

★ DELICIOUS. TIP To peel shallots easily, drop them into boiling water for 1 minute, then refresh, drain and pull away the outer skin.

Baked spinach eggs

This is a cheat's version of the nutritious and popular Eggs Florentine dish, and it makes a lovely light lunch or supper, served with crusty bread.

SERVES 2
TAKES 10 MINUTES, PLUS
10–15 MINUTES IN THE OVEN

4 tbsp ready-made tomato and chilli pasta sauce
500g bag baby spinach
Knob of butter
Freshly grated nutmeg
4 large free-range eggs
1 tbsp double cream
Crusty bread, to serve

1. Preheat the oven to 180°C/fan 160°C/gas 4 and spread the pasta sauce over the base of a baking dish.

2. Wilt the spinach in the microwave for 1–2 minutes on High, or pour a little boiling water over the spinach in a colander and drain. Mix with a knob of butter, a little salt, pepper and a grating of nutmeg. Spread the spinach over the sauce and make 4 'nests' in it.

3. Crack in the eggs. Top each with double cream and a further grating of nutmeg. Bake in the oven for 10–15 minutes.

4. Serve with good crusty bread.

Italian baked aubergines

Quickly throw together this mouthwatering Mediterranean dish; even hardened carnivores won't be able to resist.

SERVES 2
TAKES 5 MINUTES, PLUS 15 MINUTES IN THE OVEN

200g griddled aubergines (from the deli counter)
½ x 680g jar passata with onions and garlic
2 beef tomatoes, sliced
8–10 fresh basil leaves, plus extra to serve
150g mozzarella ball, drained and sliced

1. In a baking dish, layer the aubergines with the passata, tomatoes and basil leaves. Season. Top with mozzarella.

2. Bake in a preheated oven at 200°C/fan 180°C/gas 6 for 15 minutes or until bubbling. Top with fresh basil leaves to serve.

★ DELICIOUS. TIP To griddle aubergines yourself; cut them into 1cm slices lengthways and brush with oil on both sides. Cook on both sides in a hot griddle until tender and lightly charred.

Garlicky vegetable, bean and herb pot with Parmesan toasts

Experiment with different beans and herbs; why not use butter beans and cannellini beans with sage and chives instead?

SERVES 4
READY IN 30 MINUTES

2 tbsp olive oil
3 carrots, diced
2 celery sticks, diced
1 onion, roughly chopped
2 leeks, washed and sliced
150ml red wine
4 garlic cloves, crushed
400g can chopped tomatoes
200ml vegetable stock, hot
400g can flageolet beans, drained and rinsed
400g can borlotti beans, drained and rinsed
Bunch of fresh flatleaf parsley leaves, roughly chopped
Bunch of fresh oregano leaves, roughly chopped
Grated zest of 1 lemon
Slices of crusty bread, to serve
25g Parmesan, grated, to serve

1. Heat the oil in a casserole over a medium heat. Cook the carrots, celery, onion and leeks for 10 minutes, until softened. Add the wine and simmer until reduced by half.

2. Stir through the garlic, chopped tomatoes and stock. Season well and simmer for 5 minutes. Add the beans and cook for a further 5 minutes. Check the seasoning, then scatter over the fresh herbs and lemon zest.

3. Meanwhile, preheat the grill to medium and lightly toast the bread slices. Top the toasts with the grated Parmesan and grill until bubbling.

4. Divide the stew among plates and serve with the Parmesan toasts.

Aubergine and red lentil curry

A warming and spicy vegetarian dish that won't bust your budget.

SERVES 4
READY IN 40 MINUTES

- 2 tbsp vegetable oil
- 1 large aubergine, cut into chunks
- 1 green pepper, seeded and sliced
- 1 tsp mild chilli powder
- 1 onion, chopped
- 1 tsp black mustard seeds
- 2 tbsp of your favourite medium curry paste
- 150g dried red lentils
- 450ml vegetable stock, hot
- Handful of chopped fresh coriander
- Warm naan bread, to serve

1. Heat the vegetable oil in a pan over a medium heat and add the aubergine chunks and green pepper, and sprinkle with the chilli powder. Stir well to coat and cook for 8–10 minutes, until golden. Tip out on to a plate and set aside.

2. Gently fry the onion in the pan for 5 minutes, until soft. Add the mustard seeds and cook until they pop, then stir in the curry paste.

3. Stir in the lentils and stock, and simmer for 15–20 minutes, until the lentils are tender.

4. Add the roasted pepper and aubergine and heat through. Stir in a handful of chopped fresh coriander and serve with warm naan bread.

★ DELICIOUS. TIP To cut down on the cooking time, use a can of green lentils instead of dried red lentils and only a quarter of the vegetable stock. Add with the curry paste and simmer for about 5 minutes, until hot throughout.

Beany vegetable bake with garlic-bread topping

Something quick and easy for when friends come round, this clever combination of soup, beans and cheese always comes top.

SERVES 3
TAKES 10 MINUTES, PLUS 15 MINUTES IN THE OVEN

600g carton or tub of fresh vegetable soup
410g can cannellini beans, drained and rinsed
170g fresh garlic baguette
75g mature Cheddar, grated
Mixed salad, to serve

1. Preheat the oven to 200°C/fan 180°C/gas 6. Tip the soup into a saucepan. Place over a high heat, stir in the cannellini beans and heat until bubbling. Season and tip into a deep ovenproof dish, about 1.5 litres.

2. In a food processor, whiz the garlic baguette to chunky crumbs. Stir in the Cheddar and sprinkle the cheesy crumbs over the soup.

3. Bake for 15 minutes or until crisp and golden. Stand for a few minutes then spoon on to plates. Serve with a mixed salad.

Stilton and leek bread-and-butter bake

Who can resist this cheesy, savoury take on a classic British pudding?

SERVES 4
TAKES 15 MINUTES, 30–40 MINUTES IN THE OVEN, PLUS SOAKING

30g butter
2 large leeks, trimmed, cut into medium slices and washed
1 tbsp Dijon mustard
8 medium slices granary bread
3 eggs
500ml whole milk
200g vegetarian Stilton, crumbled
200g Cheddar, grated
Steamed seasonal vegetables, to serve

1. Heat 10g of the butter in a large frying pan over a medium-low heat. Add the leeks and cook gently for 6–8 minutes, stirring occasionally, until softened but not coloured. Set aside.

2. Preheat the oven to 190°C/ fan 170°C/gas 5. Thinly spread the remaining butter and the mustard on 1 side of each slice of bread. Cut each slice into quarters. In a large jug, beat together the eggs, milk and some seasoning.

3. Arrange a third of the bread, buttered-side up, in an ovenproof dish. Scatter with a third of the leeks and a third of the cheeses, then pour over a third of the milk mixture, evenly and slowly. Repeat to use up the remaining ingredients, then leave to soak for 20 minutes or so, if you have time.

4. Place the dish on a baking sheet and cook for 30–40 minutes, until risen and golden. Serve warm with steamed seasonal vegetables.

Variation For a meaty version, fry 6 chopped pork sausages until golden, then add to the leeks before layering up.

desserts

Eve's pudding

This pud is aptly named after the biblical Eve and, naturally enough, features apples. Here they're topped with a light sponge, which acts as a crust while the apples stew in their own juices beneath.

SERVES 4
TAKES 15 MINUTES, PLUS
40 MINUTES BAKING

600g cooking apples, peeled cored and roughly chopped
75g light muscovado sugar
Grated zest and juice of 1 lemon
¼ tsp ground cinnamon
100g butter
100g caster sugar, plus extra for dusting
2 large eggs
½ tsp vanilla extract
100g self-raising flour
Custard, to serve

1. Preheat the oven to 180°C/fan 160°C/gas 4. Put the apples in a large bowl and toss with the sugar, lemon zest and juice and the cinnamon. Transfer to a round 2-litre ovenproof dish and set aside.

2. Beat the butter and caster sugar in a bowl until light and fluffy. Add the eggs, 1 at a time, mixing after each addition. Mix in the vanilla, then sift in the flour and gently mix until it becomes a dropping consistency.

3. Spread the mixture over the apples and bake for 40 minutes or until the topping is cooked through and golden. Sprinkle with extra caster sugar and serve with custard.

Variation You could use fresh or canned apricots, or chunks of rhubarb for a change.

Queen of puddings

What needs to be said about this light baked pud with its spongy base, jam filling and crisp meringue topping? Just dig in and enjoy.

SERVES 6
TAKES 20 MINUTES, PLUS 25 MINUTES BAKING

50g unsalted butter, softened, plus extra for greasing
125g caster sugar
Finely grated zest of 1 lemon
600ml milk
150g fresh white breadcrumbs
4 large eggs, separated plus 1 extra white
4 tbsp raspberry jam

1. Preheat the oven to 180°C/fan 160°C/gas 4. Butter a 1-litre ovenproof dish or 4 x 300ml individual baking dishes.

2. Bring the softened butter, 25g of the sugar, the lemon zest, milk and a pinch of salt to a gentle simmer in a pan. Add the breadcrumbs and set aside, stirring often, until thickened.

3. Stir the egg yolks into the mixture and spoon into the prepared dish/dishes. Bake for about 15 minutes or until just set.

4. Heat the jam in a small pan until runny, then carefully spread over the top of the pudding/s – being careful not to break the surface.

5. Whisk the egg whites and remaining sugar for about 4 minutes in a heatproof bowl set over a pan of gently simmering water until the sugar has dissolved (check by rubbing a little between your fingers – if it is still grainy, beat for a bit longer) and the whites have formed soft peaks. Spoon over the top of the pudding and swirl to form peaks. Bake for about 10 minutes, until the meringue is lightly browned and crisp. Serve immediately.

Apricot buttermilk cake

A soft, creamy fruity pud that's perfect for the summer. Use fresh apricots for the ultimate fresh, moist cake.

SERVES 12
TAKES 20 MINUTES, 40–45 MINUTES BAKING, PLUS COOLING

175g butter, very soft, plus extra for greasing
200g self-raising flour
150g ground almonds
200g golden caster sugar
142ml buttermilk
3 large free-range eggs, beaten
1 tsp vanilla extract
Finely grated zest of 1 lemon
6 ripe apricots, halved and stoned
2 tbsp mild runny honey
50g flaked almonds

For the honey cream
142ml carton double cream
150ml Greek-style yogurt
4 tbsp mild runny honey

1. Preheat the oven to 180°C/fan 160°C/ gas 4. Grease and line a 30cm x 23cm x 5cm baking tin with baking paper. Whiz together all the dry ingredients in a food processor. Add the butter, buttermilk, eggs, vanilla extract and lemon zest, and pulse until combined.

2. Pour into the tin, level, and arrange the apricots on top, cut-side up. Drizzle with honey and sprinkle with the almonds. Bake for 40–45 minutes, then set aside to cool for 20 minutes.

3. Meanwhile, whip the cream, yogurt and honey together until thickened. Serve the cake with the honey cream.

ITALIA

Pear, blackberry and eau de vie flaugnarde

This recipe needs perfectly ripe pears. If you can't find them, poach pear slices in a sugar syrup or sauté in butter until tender.

SERVES 4
TAKES 20 MINUTES, PLUS
30 MINUTES BAKING

3 ripe pears
150g blackberries
4 tbsp pear eau de vie or Calvados
25g unsalted butter, plus extra for greasing

For the batter
150ml milk
142ml carton double cream
1 tsp vanilla extract
3 eggs
125g caster sugar
50g plain flour, sifted
Icing sugar, to serve

1. Preheat the oven to 180°C/fan 160°C/gas 4. Halve and core the pears, then cut lengthways into 5mm slices. Put immediately into a bowl with the blackberries. Pour over the eau de vie or Calvados and toss well to cover.

2. Make the batter. Mix together the milk, cream and vanilla extract. Butter a gratin dish (metal or cast-iron is best as it conducts the heat well). Using a slotted spoon, arrange the pears and blackberries in the dish and add any eau de vie left behind to the batter mixture.

3. In a large bowl, whisk together the eggs, sugar and a pinch of salt until the mixture triples in volume and is pale and fluffy – you need a powerful beater. Fold in the flour, then add the milk mixture.

4. Pour the batter over the pear slices, dot with the butter and bake in the oven for 30 minutes, until the batter is set. Remove from the oven and set aside for 5 minutes. Sift a little icing sugar over the top before serving warm.

Pear and cranberry clafoutis

Clafoutis is a traditional French dessert, usually made with cherries. Try autumn fruits for a delicious change.

SERVES 4
TAKES 10 MINUTES, PLUS 20–25 MINUTES BAKING

3 eggs
2 egg yolks
75g golden caster sugar
30g plain flour
225ml milk
½ tsp vanilla extract
1 tsp butter, for greasing
2 pears
100g ready-to-eat dried cranberries
2 tbsp flaked almonds
Icing sugar, to dust

1. Preheat the oven to 190°C/fan 170°C/gas 5. Beat together the eggs, egg yolks and caster sugar in a large bowl until pale and thick. Fold in the flour, then the milk and vanilla, beating to a smooth batter.

2. Butter an 18cm x 26cm ovenproof dish. Peel the pears and cut into quarters, removing the cores. Arrange in the dish and scatter with the cranberries. Pour the batter over the fruit and sprinkle with almonds. Bake for 20–25 minutes until golden and the custard is just set. Dust with icing sugar and serve warm.

Black Forest cherry dessert

All the wonderful flavours of cherries, brandy and chocolate in an instant dessert.

SERVES 4
TAKES 10 MINUTES, PLUS COOLING

250g fresh or frozen cherries
2 tbsp icing sugar
3 tbsp cherry brandy, brandy, kirsch or any fruit liqueur
200g chocolate sponge cake or 4 chocolate muffins
250ml good-quality vanilla ice cream
50g plain chocolate, roughly grated

1. Place the cherries in a pan with the sugar and brandy or liqueur. Cook gently over a medium heat for 5–6 minutes until the cherries are softened but still hold their shape. Remove from the heat and cool.

2. Slice the cake into 4 pieces, then divide these or the muffins among serving bowls or cups. Spoon over half of the juice from the cooked cherries, then top with scoops of ice cream, the cherries and more of their juice. Finish with a scattering of the grated chocolate.

Plums roasted with sloe gin

Roasting plums with the gin of their wild sloe cousins is delicious. You could swap the gin for another sticky drink, if you like, such as port or crème de cassis.

SERVES 4
TAKES 15 MINUTES, 15–20 MINUTES BAKING, PLUS COOLING

12 plums, halved and stoned
150ml sloe gin (see tip) or use Gordon's Sloe Gin
Juice of 1 orange, plus a little extra
60g golden caster sugar

1. Preheat the oven to 200°C/fan 180°C/gas 6. Put the plums in a large roasting tin, cut-side up. Mix together the gin and orange juice, and pour over the fruit. Sprinkle with the sugar and bake for 15–20 minutes, until tender.

2. Using a slotted spoon, transfer to a large dish to cool. Put the roasting tin over a high heat on the hob. Bring the remaining juices to the boil and cook for 3–4 minutes or until reduced and syrupy. Cool, then pour over the cooled plums.

★ DELICIOUS. TIP To make your own sloe gin, wash and prick 450g sloes with a fork and combine in a large Kilner jar with 450g sugar and a 70cl bottle of gin. Turn the jar every day for the first week or so to dissolve the sugar and colour the gin evenly. Keep for at least 3 months before serving – ideally, pick the sloes in September and enjoy the gin at Christmas.

Eccles cakes baked apples

These mouthwatering apples have the spicy flavour of Eccles cakes without the fatty pastry.

SERVES 4
TAKES 15 MINUTES, 40–45 MINUTES BAKING, PLUS COOLING

- 50g butter
- 50g light muscovado sugar
- 50g dark muscovado sugar
- 250g currants
- 1 tsp ground allspice
- 1 tsp freshly grated nutmeg
- ½ tsp ground cinnamon
- Pinch of ground cloves
- Finely grated zest of 1 lemon and 1 tbsp fresh lemon juice
- 4 large Bramley apples (about 300g each)
- Custard, thick cream or vanilla ice cream, to serve

1. Melt the butter in a medium saucepan over a gentle heat. Add both the sugars, remove from the heat and stir to remove any lumps. Stir in the currants, spices and lemon zest and juice, and set aside to cool completely. As the mixture cools, the dried fruit will absorb most of the buttery juices, the rest will solidify around it.

2. Preheat the oven to 180°C/fan 160°C/gas 4. Core the apples using an apple corer then, using a swivel peeler or a small, sharp knife, open up the cavities a little more until they measure about 3cm across. Slice a little off the base of each apple, if necessary, so that they sit flat, then score horizontally around the middle of each apple just to cut through the skin to stop them bursting.

3. Place the apples in a shallow baking dish and stuff the cavities with the filling, piling any excess on the top. Spoon 2 tablespoons water into the dish and bake in the oven for 20 minutes. Remove and cover the apples loosely with foil. Bake for a further 20–25 minutes or until the apples are soft to the centre when pierced with the tip of a sharp knife.

4. Serve the baked apples immediately with the syrupy juices from the dish and some custard, thick cream or vanilla ice cream.

★ DELICIOUS. TIP This dish should be served immediately, as the apples will collapse if left to stand.

Chocolate sponge pudding

You can enjoy this chocolate pud hot, with cream, custard or a good ice cream. But it also keeps well and tastes great cold.

SERVES 6–8
TAKES 10 MINUTES, 35–40 MINUTES BAKING, PLUS COOLING

225g unsalted butter, plus extra for greasing
100g plain bitter (70% cocoa solids) chocolate
2 large free-range eggs
250g soft dark brown sugar
200g plain flour
1 tsp baking powder
1 tbsp strong coffee (instant is fine)
Unsweetened cream, to serve

1. Preheat the oven to 180°C/fan 160°C/ gas 4. Dice the butter and break the chocolate into chunks. Put in a bowl over a pan of simmering water and gently melt. Don't stir, as it is easy to overwork bitter chocolate.

2. In a bowl, beat the eggs and sugar until pale(ish) and smooth. Fold in the chocolate mix, then the flour and baking powder, and beat until smooth. Finally, beat in the coffee and 250ml boiling water. You now have a smooth batter. Line a 18cm-square tin with butter and baking paper, and pour in the batter. Bake for 35–40 minutes, then test by inserting a skewer into the middle. It might not come out clean, but some stickiness is ok.

3. Cool for a good 20–30 minutes before serving with unsweetened cream for a delicious contrast.

Bread pudding

Not to be confused with bread and butter pudding, this is a dense, sticky affair. Served hot, it's fantastic with custard or ice cream. Make it in a sandwich tin and serve pieces of it like pie.

SERVES 6–8
TAKES 10 MINUTES, PLUS 30 MINUTES BAKING, PLUS SOAKING

3 tbsp brandy
100g soft pitted prunes, halved
100g juicy sultanas
8 stale sourdough bread slices, crusts removed
300ml whole milk
50g butter, melted, plus extra for greasing
1 large free-range egg
100g soft dark brown sugar
Grated zest of 1 orange
½ tbsp freshly grated nutmeg
2 tbsp caster sugar

1. Warm the brandy in a small pan. Add the prunes and sultanas, warm through, then cover and remove from the heat. Set aside for 10 minutes to infuse.

2. Meanwhile, preheat the oven to 180°C/fan 160°C/gas 4. Break up the bread and mix it with the milk and butter in a bowl. Squash the bread between your fingers until all the milk has been absorbed. Beat in the egg, dark brown sugar, orange zest and nutmeg. Add the fruit and any brandy from the pan.

3. Grease and line a 20cm-round loose-bottomed sandwich tin with butter and baking paper. Press in the pudding and sprinkle the top with the caster sugar. Bake for 30 minutes or until just set in the middle and a little crunchy on top. Serve hot or pour on a little brandy and flambé it, Christmas pudding-style.

Blueberry sponge slice

If you have any leftover sponge slices after serving this decadent dessert, they will keep in the fridge for a couple of days.

MAKES 6 SLICES
TAKES 10 MINUTES, PLUS FREEZING

2 x 225g punnets blueberries
Juice of 1 lemon
150g icing sugar, plus extra to dust
1 small Madeira cake
200g soft cream cheese
250g tub mascarpone
3 tbsp Marsala, Madeira or sweet sherry
50g toasted flaked almonds

1. Place the blueberries in a pan with the lemon juice and 75g of the icing sugar. Heat gently for about 5 minutes or until the blueberries are beginning to burst and you have a lovely sauce. Remove from the heat.

2. Meanwhile, slice the Madeira cake lengthways into 3 pieces and arrange in the base of a 25cm x 15cm shallow roasting tin or dish. Spread the blueberries over the top and spoon on the juices to soak into the sponge.

3. Place the cream cheese, mascarpone and Marsala, Madeira or sherry and the remaining icing sugar in a bowl and beat together well until smooth. Spread the cream-cheese mixture over the cooled blueberries.

4. Place in the freezer for about 20 minutes – this will help it set quickly.

5. Sprinkle with the flaked almonds and dust with icing sugar to serve.

additional tips

Choosing the best cuts of meat for slow cooking

Slow cooking and one-pot cooking are becoming more popular because these methods are a convenient way of cooking inexpensive cuts of meat to create dishes that offer superb depth of flavour.

Chicken is ideal for one-pot cooking, but whatever meat you prefer, it's best to choose the correct cut for the job. Here's a breakdown of which cuts are best, plus a few handy cooking tips.

Cuts of pork

Spare rib and hand

Both of these joints can be successfully braised. Brown them first to give some colour, then place on a bed of vegetables together with a little liquid, and cook in a covered casserole in the oven. Or dice for use in casseroles. Slow cooking will make the meat meltingly tender.

Loin

Cooking this cut as above can also help keep what can be a slightly drier cut of meat nicely moist. This joint will also give much neater slices.

Chump end

When diced, it is ideal for stews, curries and casseroles, and tends to be more tender than leg.

Belly

Although this is quite a fatty cut, it can still be very successfully slow-cooked. The Chinese love to give it this treatment. During cooking, the excess fat melts and rises to the surface, where it can be skimmed away before serving.

Tenderloin and leg

Both of these cuts are commonly diced and used in casseroles and stews as they provide lean, well-textured meat, which retains its shape during cooking.

Cuts of beef

Shin and leg

Inexpensive cuts with bags of flavour, both of these are made up of very lean muscle.

Chuck and blade

This is what most recipes mean when they call for braising steak. It is a very tasty cut of beef that can be sliced or diced.

Middle ribs

When boned and rolled, this is a beautiful joint for pot-roasting. It can also be sliced or diced for use in casseroles.

Brisket

This is a cylindrical joint that gives nice neat slices when carved. Because it comes from the belly of the animal it can sometimes be fatty, but this is what adds to the flavour of the stock during cooking.

Short ribs

Traditionally an American cut that is often called 'oven-busters' over here, short ribs are becoming quite trendy. Slowly braised in wine or beer with vegetables and lots of aromatics, they become very tender and almost velvety in texture when slow-cooked, with a fantastic flavour.

Minced neck and flank

Mince made from the tougher cuts of meat is best used in dishes requiring slow cooking. Mince from a prime cut, such as tail of the fillet, is usually reserved for serving raw in dishes such as steak tartare.

Skirt

This cut of beef is usually reserved for slow cooking in either steak and kidney pudding or Cornish pasties.

Silverside

A neat, cylindrical joint, silverside is ideally suited to braising or pot-roasting.

Oxtail

Oxtail is a tough off-cut of beef that requires long, slow cooking to become tender. Because it is a cut of meat still on the bone – and also comes with quite a lot of fat, cartilage and marrow – it contains a staggering amount of flavour. It is the cut to use for osso bucco.

Cuts of lamb

Scrag end

This cut is tough and has less meat, but tons of flavour. It is excellent slow-cooked in soups and stews, either on or off the bone.

Middle neck or neck

The middle neck or neck can be cut into 2.5cm slices, and is traditionally used for slow cooking on the bone in dishes such as Lancashire hotpot (see page 34).

Neck fillets

Although these are ideal for all methods of fast cooking, they also produce beautifully tender meat when slow-cooked. It also takes a lot less time to cook them in a stew – no more than 45 minutes.

Boned and diced shoulder or leg

Both are perfect in stews or casseroles. Meat from the shoulder needs to be trimmed of excess fat first. The leg gives neater, leaner pieces of meat than the shoulder, but both are meltingly tender and have fantastic flavour.

Leg and shoulder joints

These cuts are great slow-roasted in a covered pan for many hours, until the meat is literally falling off the bone.

Lamb shanks

A lean, gelatinous well-flavoured meat, lamb shanks are ideal for long, slow cooking, producing melt-in-the-mouth results.

Chump

This cut is a solid, lean well-flavoured meat that is great for dicing and long, slow cooking.

Breast

Despite being quite a fatty cut, it can still be slow-cooked very successfully, and becomes wonderfully tender. Skim off any excess fat before serving.

Tips for slow cooking

1. Making a slow-cooked dish the day before will improve the flavour immensely. Chill it overnight, then reheat and simmer gently for the briefest time possible before serving.

2. Covering the dish with a tight-fitting lid or foil is also very important, especially with some braised dishes in which the meat is cooked in relatively little liquid. It stops the sauce reducing too much.

3. When seasoning slow-cooked dishes, do so lightly at the beginning. This method encourages reduction of the liquid, so the sauce can become much more concentrated.

4. Brown the meat first; cook it in small batches, if necessary, to maintain a high heat in the pan. This caramelises some of the juices in the pan, adding to the flavour, so you should do it in the pot in which you will cook the rest of the dish, ideally a cast-iron, flameproof casserole with a tight-fitting lid.

5. Cook the meat at the correct temperature at the start of cooking. The liquid in the pan should not be allowed to bubble at all vigorously, but just tremble in the centre of the pot. This lets the meat become meltingly tender but not fall apart.

6. If you need to toss the meat in a little flour before browning, make sure it is not overly wet and that only a light dusting clings to the outside. This will give your meat a good colour.

Index

Picture and recipe credits

Harper Collins would like to thank the following contributors for providing photographs:

Steve Baxter p13, p15, p21, p23, p25, p35, p47, p63, p71, p73, p115, p123, p153, p165, p175; Vanessa Courtier p57; Tara Fisher p133; Jonathan Gregson p43, p69, p103, p117, p120–121, p137, p143, p158–9, p173, p177, p179, p192; Richard Jung p41, p49, p127, p161, p163, p167, p171; David Loftus p17, p139; Gareth Morgans p79, p91, p93; Lis Parsons pp30–31, p45, p65, p75, p83, p119; Craig Robertson p10, p19, p27, p29, p33, p39, p55, p59, p67, p71, p77, p81, p85, p87, p98–9, p101, p105, p107, p109, p125, p135, p140–141, p145, p147, p149, p151, p157; Brett Stevens p37; Lucinda Symons p89; Karen Thomas p61, p95; Philip Webb p111, p129, p131; Stuart West p113, p155; Kate Whitaker p51, p97, p169; Rob White p51, p53

With thanks, too, for all the following for creating the recipes for delicious. magazine which are used in this book:

Kate Belcher p38, p50, p52, p54, p76, p102, p142, p154; Katie Bishop p36; Angela Boggiano p16, p18, p24, p26, p28, p50, p56, p66, p70, p80, p96, p108, p124, p132, p138, p146, p148, p160, p162; Matthew Drennan p12, p14, p20, p22, p92; Jill Dupleix p168, p170
Silvana Franco p32, p48, p84, p86, p134, p156; Alice Hart p64, p104, p106, p144, p164; Sal Henley p110, p128, p130; Diana Henry p166; Debbie Major p74, p82, p174; Kim Morphew p118; Tom Norrington-Davies p40, p44, p68, p116, p126, p136, p172, p176, p178; Carol Tennant p88; Lizzie Webb-Wilson p34, p46, p60, p62, p70, p72, p94, p114, p122, p152; Lucy Williams p58, p100, p112, p150; Mitzie Wilson p42, p78, p90